GOD CAN DO MORE WITH OUR RELINQUISHED CONTROL,
THAN WE CAN DO BY HOLDING ONTO IT.

# OUT OF CONTROL

DEBORAH HILTON

# Out of Control

Copyright © Deborah Hilton, 2020

All rights reserved. No part of this publication may be reproduced, stored in or introduced into a database and retrieval system or transmitted in any form or any means (electronic, mechanical, photocopying, recording or otherwise) without the prior written permission of the publisher.

All Scripture quotations, unless otherwise indicated, are taken from the Holy Bible, New International Version®, NIV®. Copyright ©1973, 1978, 1984, 2011 by Biblica, Inc.TM Used by permission of Zondervan. All rights reserved.

Scripture quotations marked (NLT) are taken from the Holy Bible, New Living Translation, copyright ©1996, 2004, 2007, 2013, 2015 by Tyndale House Foundation. Used by permission of Tyndale House Publishers, Inc., Carol Stream, Illinois 60188. All rights reserved.

Scripture quotations marked (TLB) are taken from The Living Bible copyright © 1971. Used by permission of Tyndale House Publishers, Inc., Carol Stream, Illinois 60188. All rights reserved.

Scripture quotations marked (NKJV) are taken from the New King James Version. Copyright © 1982 by Thomas Nelson, Inc. Used by permission. All rights reserved.

Scripture quotations marked (AMP) are taken from the Amplified® Bible, Copyright © 1954, 1958, 1962, 1964, 1965, 1987 by The Lockman Foundation Used by permission.

Scripture quotations marked (NASB) are taken from the New American Standard Bible®, Copyright © 1960, 1962, 1963, 1968, 1971, 1972, 1973, 1975, 1977, 1995 by The Lockman Foundation Used by permission..

Scripture quotations marked (CEV) are taken from the Contemporary English Version Copyright © 1991, 1992, 1995 by American Bible Society. Used by Permission.

Scripture quotations marked (MSG) are taken from THE MESSAGE. Copyright © by Eugene H. Peterson 1993, 1994, 1995, 1996, 2000, 2001, 2002. Used by permission of NavPress. All rights reserved. Represented by Tyndale House Publishers, Inc.

ISBN: 978-0-9946362-2-5

Edited by Jillian Brady

Cover Concept by Josh Hilton
Cover Design by Andrew Thomas
Layout Design by Cherie Mountney

Photo of Deborah Hilton by Paul Hilton
Published by Deborah Hilton
2020

Printed by IngramSpark, Lightning Source Inc.

# My deepest appreciation to...

### PAUL

You are my greatest fan and encourager. I am blessed beyond measure to call you husband. Thank you for believing in me and always cheering me on with the dreams and goals in my heart I want to pursue, and this my second book, is no exception.

### BELINDA

Thank you, Belinda, my daughter, for allowing me to use a small part of your story so others know they don't walk alone on difficult roads.

### JOSH

Thank you, Josh, my son, for allowing me to use a small part of your story for others to know God will speak to you regardless of the season you are in. Thank you also for the creative concept for the front cover of this book.

### THE FIVE BRAVE SOULS

Thank you, to you five wonderful people who were willing share your stories. Thank you for being brave enough to allow others to get a glimpse into your lives of struggle and your journey towards wholeness. I know your stories will be healing for so many who read this book.

### JILLIAN BRADY

Thank you once again Jill for pouring over the pages of this book with your editing eyes to fine tune the little things that make a difference.

## CHERIE MOUNTNEY

Thank you, Cherie for working with me on getting the layout just right. Your graphic eye has made this book look as good as it does. I couldn't have gone to print without you.

## ANDREW THOMAS

Thank you for taking the creative concept to design a cover that captures the message of this book.

## OTHERS

I am so grateful to all my wonderful friends who encouraged me to write. Never did I imagine that I would become an author, but God knew. I also want to thank Julia Britto and Michelle Applegate for being willing to take time to glean the pages of my book to look for those little things. 'Is it one dot or three?' 'Is it a colon or semi colon?' I know from experience though, you can edit, edit, edit
and still find mistakes.

## THE HOLY SPIRIT

There are no adequate words to describe how grateful and indebted I am to you. You are the true writer of this book. Your whisper to my spirit every day that I opened my computer, directed me on what to include and what to leave out. May Your anointing be on this book to bring healing and wholeness to many.

# What others are saying about 'Out of Control'

This book brings an important message written from a deep well of faith and personal experience. I still remember my first conversation with Deb, it was more than 10 years ago now, and it was life changing! I was in that space of confusion and uncertainty many of us find ourselves in along our journey's with Christ. Confronted by a mountain sized problem that I just could not look away from, I was dwarfed by my own inadequacy in comparison to it, yet I could not escape the passion of God's heart to see answers delivered. I felt 'Out of Control', and I didn't like it! Deb's words to me in that moment not only bought understanding, they bought wisdom and faith. She looked me straight in the eyes and said, *'It sounds like God is birthing something powerful through you.* ***You don't need to know everything, just take the first step and trust God.'*** The authority of Deb's voice came from her own wealth of personal experience in living life 'Out of Control', but certain in God, and her confidence, gave me the confidence to take my important first step.

Get ready!! The message of this book will give you the confidence to take your hands off the 'wheel of control' and instead trust God, step by step.

**JANINE KUBALA**
Founder Esther's Voice.
Director Kubala Ministries.
Senior Pastor C3 Believe.

Control! Control! Control! We can all have a desire to control things in our world, whether that be situations, circumstances or people. We can be 'born' with a strong desire to control, or 'gain' it through the 'conditioning' of society, but control is something that is part of our lives. In navigating much of life, we need to use control in areas such as our emotions, habits, maybe spending patterns. This is the positive use of control. However, when we are 'out of control', our lives, and the lives of others around us, can be impacted negatively. Also, sometimes without any fault of our own, life can just get 'out of control'. Even then, we can feel the need to try and 'control' the situation, lest our world fall apart.

In her book 'OUT OF CONTROL', Deb in an honest, transparent and revealing manner, shares some of her own personal journey of the need to be in control, for fear of life being 'out of control', to a freedom of knowing that God is actually in control and He can be trusted when we hand control over to Him. Deb also gives us practical keys to gaining freedom from the 'controlling' grip of CONTROL. This is a must read book.

**JOEL CHELLIAH**
Senior Pastor Centrepoint Church - Perth, Western Australia.
ACC Western Australia, State President.

Deb Hilton's latest book 'Out of Control' takes us on a very personal journey. It's vulnerable and candid. Not every leader of Deb's stature would be comfortable with this level of transparency, but her honesty gives the reader permission to take steps, that will ultimately lead them on a path to freedom.

Discovering the unfailing truth that God is God, and then yielding to His Lordship, was life changing for the author and several others. This could be the place where you discover yourself and your God in a whole new way.

**WAYNE AND LYN ALCORN**
Senior Pastors Hope Centre - Brisbane, Australia.

Deb Hilton has ministered for many years as a highly effective missionary. She was previously engaged in areas of pastoral ministry. Her passion to help others in need has steered her into places of great need, where her compassion and skill have enabled her to bring real help to multitudes of hurting and desperate people.

In the light of Deb's evident compassion, this book is a courageous and honest sharing of her life, revealing to us her life journey with her lessons learned in a life of compassion. She openly shares her sense of needing to be in control so as to enable her to better help others. This is the challenge of compassion. Do we take control to help others? How can we compassionately help others without being controlling?

The insights shared by Deb are priceless. Her insights are practical and spiritual. She shows us how we can effectively deal with our issues and still exercise our compassion with faith as we help others without taking control.

Thank you Deb, this book I'm sure will help many to be more effective in their compassionate helping of others.

**ALUN DAVIES**
President Australian Christian Churches International (ACCI).
Vice President Australian Christian Churches (ACC).


I think God is sending a message to all of us right now and it goes something like this, 'I am God, you can trust me! Throw your life into my hands and watch me do things in you and through you that may never have happened if you maintained the control of your life.' OUT OF CONTROL will be a life defining read that will help you 'let go', and truly experience life in its fullness with Jesus in the driver's seat of your life. Enjoy.

**JULIA A'BELL**
Senior Pastor RVTLS, Revitalise Church - Sydney, Australia.
ACC National Women's Ministry Leader.


What area of your life is out of control that you would most like to control? Or who in your life right now would you most like to control? Let's be honest, we are all control freaks, if only in regards to our lives. We want to control our lives rather than letting God who created us, loves us and has a perfect plan for us, shape and mould our lives. When we overestimate our ability to control a situation, we underestimate the power of God.

Deb Hilton has a great story to tell having been placed in numerous circumstances where she had little or no control. She learned to let go and trust God. These powerful life lessons are available to you in this book. You will discover that you don't always have the power to control, but you still can trust God and surrender to Him and watch Him work a miracle.

**SEAN STANTON**
Senior Pastor Life Unlimited Church - Canberra, Australia.
ACC National Secretary, Australia.

I believe this book is going to greatly help you to realise God is wanting to totally free you from the weight of being in control of situations and relationships, without losing any sense of acting responsibly. Life circumstances unfortunately can easily throw us into the default mode of 'control' as we must feel secure. The more we try to be in control, the more we fear losing control. The more we fear losing control, the more we want to be in control. At the core of it is TRUST - trust in yourself or trust in God. Trusting in God isn't a one-time event – it is a daily choice. As you read this book and allow God to take you on a journey of releasing your hold to Him, you will discover a wonderful rest and freedom that enables you to actually start enjoying life!

**LYNDA STANTON**
Senior Pastor Life Unlimited Church - Canberra, Australia.

I've known Deb Hilton for over 20 years. I would count her and her husband Paul as friends. After her first incredible and well-received book Deb Hilton is back with a second. Deb is passionate, articulate and the real deal. She's a 'tell it like it is' Aussie girl and her words carry a powerful punch. *'Out of Control'* is a deeply personal book with Deb doing what she does best; telling riveting stories and follows up her narratives with astute biblical applications. Deb's new book gives hope and helps people see life realistically, even when life feels out of control. This is a timely book. Her maturity, clarity and insight are inspiring. She has become a voice to this generation. This book is indeed a must-read.

**TOM RAWLS**
Senior Pastor Proclaimers Church - Norwich, England.

Some books are alive – they become companions to us though different seasons of our lives. Sometimes they comfort us to remind us that we are not alone in our struggles. Other times they help us navigate a way out when we are stuck. This book will be one of those companions, as you journey through whatever form your control challenge takes. Deb and the friends she mentions in this book are ones we can look up to, who have traversed the way ahead of us, and found their way OUT OF CONTROL. As a couple, we have been looking up to Deb and her husband Paul for over 20 years. They are the real deal! Their tenacious example of following the call of God as a family and their timely words of wisdom have inspired and guided us in our own ministry journey across the world.

**KIRK & TRACEE MCATEAR**
Senior Pastors Connect Church - Birmingham, UK.
AOG Great Britain Missions Director.


Deborah is a well-respected leader, a beautiful author and most importantly, a wonderful woman of God. Her new book 'Out of Control' confronts the well concealed, self-reliant attitude of 'Yep, God, don't worry, I've got this one…'. Deborah will take you through the journeys of other men and women, including her own, to find freedom from the burden of being in control. Instead, you will discover the joy of being responsible. Just responsible, nothing more. Jesus' words 'My yoke is easy and my burden is light' will come to life when you learn to uproot the need to control and replace it with the appropriate reactions and responses, fully trusting God, who is our true burden carrier.

**RACHEL MIQUEL DUFOUR**
Director of S.A.M Ministries.
Pastor, Therapist, Author - Colorado, USA.

# CONTENTS

FOREWORD

INTRODUCTION

PART 1  |  Joanna's Story
1. Who in the world is Joanna
2. Revealing Joanna

PART 2  |  My Story
3. Burden Carrier
4. Our Filter System
5. Lessons learnt but easily forgotten
6. The straw that broke the camel's back
7. Wising up

PART 3  |  Their Story
8. You are not alone
9. Out of the ashes
10. He is more than enough
11. Captain Underpants
12. Peacekeeper
13. Letting God take care of the curve balls
14. The root of control
15. COVID-19

PART 4  |  Your Story
16. Adjusting your sails
17. Your tool kit
18. Balance and trust

DON'T SKIP THE EPILOGUE

REFERENCE NOTES

# FOREWARD

I have known Deb since she was 16. I met her on the way to a youth camp, and following that weekend, along with a bunch of other guys and girls, we hung out together most weekends as a 'group' within our church youth group. We did everything together. It didn't take too long before I started to take more than a 'hanging out with the mates' kind of interest in Deb. Besides being 'more than pleasant on the eye', I was attracted to her bubbly, outgoing personality. We increasingly spent more time together, fell in love and were married.

As I write this foreward, we have just celebrated our 44th wedding anniversary. I mention this to say that I hold a unique position in Deb's life. Of all the people on the planet, I know her more than anyone else. I know her idiosyncrasies and habits, like the fact that you must always use the same coloured pegs on each article of clothing you hang on the clothesline. I didn't learn the 'extreme' importance of that until we had been married for about 10 years. I know her likes and dislikes, her goals and dreams, but also her anxieties and fears. I have seen her ecstatic about exciting things happening in her life, but also the heartbreak over situations that have happened in just doing life.

> ...we have a God who can do more with our relinquished control, than we can by holding on to it

In doing life with Deb, what I have seen is how she has learnt to navigate many of the challenges thrown her (our) way, and she has navigated them well. However, there have also been situations and times where Deb has felt things were Out Of Control, and if she didn't take CONTROL of them, then her world would fall apart.

OUT OF CONTROL, is a deeply personal book written out of a fairly recent period of trauma, grief and heartache for us as a family, a period where Deb would have loved to have been able to 'control' or 'fix', but realised that she could not fix any one of the challenging events. They were all out of her control. This lead her on a journey of discovering that we don't always have control of situations, and we don't need to, as we have a God who can do more with our relinquished control, than we can by holding on to it. In a brutally honest and transparent way, Deb shares her journey with God through this recent 'Out Of Control' period and takes us back to a time in her childhood where her need to be in control stemmed from. She also gives us some practical tools that will take us on a path to freedom. Freedom from the grip of needing to be in control, to allowing God to take control, knowing He can be trusted with our lives.

Deb wrote this book for YOU. Enjoy!

**Paul Hilton**
Deb's husband & greatest fan

# INTRODUCTION

Well here I am again, writing another book. Who would have thought? A non-reader becoming an author! Doesn't make sense really, does it? Or does it? Isn't it just like God to choose the unqualified to do something significant through them? To choose someone others may never consider, who only see him or her as completely inexperienced and therefore crosses them off the list. Yet Almighty God, our Heavenly Father, searches throughout the earth looking for someone whose only qualification needs to be a heart fully surrendered to Him. When He finds that one, He says, 'You, I choose you'.

How do I know this; that I am one of the unqualified that God has chosen? Growing up in a dysfunctional home; bullied at school; just scraping through to grade 10 before getting out of school – or what I called an institution - I felt very unqualified for a lot of things.

Now, this unqualified girl is stamped qualified, capable, eligible and certified by the One and Only Father God. If you read my last book, 'Just say YES,' you would have gained a glimpse into my heart which desires deeply to see others completely set free from restraint to fulfill their calling and trust God in their journey. To know that they too are qualified.

This, my second book, OUT OF CONTROL, is a totally different book to my first. At this milestone age of 60 and some months, (it's just a number everyone), I have had many life experiences and learnt numerous lessons from those experiences. So, it is my responsibility to share these in the hope that it helps someone else out there, maybe you, and fast tracks your learning to get on with living a full life that is whole, and running your race without restraint.

So here we go.

OUT OF CONTROL. What do you associate with this statement, 'Out Of Control'? I am sure you have heard people say, 'She is completely out of control,' or 'He has totally lost it!' This is usually what we think of when that statement is voiced. However, the 'out of control' I am talking about is when, at times, you find yourself dropping the proverbial juggling balls, in the life that you believe you were meant to be in control of.

The dictionary defines control as: to exercise authoritative or dominating influence over; ability to manage; to hold in restraint.

Whatever we personally brand control as, to some degree, we all want it. We want to know that everything is safe and secure in our world, which is both a normal and natural expectation for our life.

For those of us who are control freaks however, it goes beyond the average expectation. We black belts of control, feel it is our duty, our responsibility, a burden put upon us to keep everything organized, flowing, happy, drama free and on track at all times. We make it our full-time occupation, because heaven forbid, if we let go, our world, and possibly *the* world, would cave in, causing us to become anxious, helpless and 'out of control'. If we can keep all we have claimed responsibility for, in a nice neat package, which is easy to govern and regulate, then our life will be just fine. Those of us who have tendencies to over control, whether that is a conscious action or an unconscious propensity, have this false sense of belief, that because we have made it our responsibility, we don't have the luxury to let go of that control.

Does any of this sound familiar to you? If so, then you need this book. I need this book, haha!! I wrote it out of first-hand knowledge and experience of being one who has always felt the need to be in control of my world lest we die!! Sounds crazy ay? But how true it is for so many of us.

My heart and my prayer is that as we journey together on this pathway of moving from being control freaks to living a balanced, responsible, and faith-filled life, we will discover that our Father God is big enough, capable enough, devoted enough, more than enough and quite able enough to hold all things together in the palm of His hand.

Are you ready to give, 'letting go and letting God' a chance? If you have said YES, and I hope you have, then let's get changing!

# Part 1: JOANNA'S STORY

# 1
## WHO IN THE WORLD IS JOANNA?

I'm glad you asked. Joanna is one of my favourite Bible characters because she is almost an unknown and yet she played such a significant role in the life of Jesus while He walked this earth. Most people don't even realise she is in the Bible and I can already hear you rustling through your own Bible or scrolling through chapters on your iPad, iPhone or whatever other iThing you own, or more than likely, 'Googling' her name to find this woman called Joanna, all the while asking yourself this question, 'Is Joanna actually in the Bible?'

If I said I was going to write about the life of Queen Esther, those of you who read the Bible would probably say to me; 'Deb, take a seat, I can recite her story backwards to you, we know Esther,' and you would be right. Even if you don't know her from the Bible, you may know of her from the movie made about her, called 'The Book of Esther,' made in 2013. Many people quote her story as an encouragement to those who are questioning whether their life is making a difference, reminding them that they are in the right place, at the right time, for the season they are in. For Queen Esther, God had moved all the chess pieces, so to speak, in order for her to be chosen as the new wife of King Ahasuerus, the king of Persia. This led her to be positioned for her ultimate calling, a place of influence, to save the Jewish people, her people, from being wiped out. The plan to destroy the Jews came about after a law was put in place to have the people in that nation bow down to the King's servants, however Esther's uncle Mordecai, a Jew, would not. Haman, the chief servant, got angry and asked the king to make a law to wipe out the Jews in that nation. Queen Esther got word of this plot and had her people pray and fast, as did she, prior to her bravely going before her King to plead for the lives of her people. She succeeded in this quest and hence, the famous quote associated with Queen Esther was birthed: 'And who knows but that you have come to your royal position for such a time as this?' Esther 4:14

What a great story. However, this chapter is not about Queen Esther but rather about another significant player in biblical history; and her name is Joanna and yes, she is in the Bible.

I discovered this amazing woman while I was preparing to preach. Our pastor had asked those of us on the preaching roster to choose a New Testament character to speak about and immediately I thought, I want to find someone no one knows, and it was on this quest I found the beautiful Joanna.

To find her, you will need to look carefully, because she can easily be overlooked. Even if you have read about her, you can be forgiven for failing to notice her significance and her noteworthiness. Joanna is mentioned just four times in the New Testament, and only very briefly, but as you pause to take a closer look, you will discover a woman of incredible character and distinction. As you dig deep, you will find a woman, who through a life-changing encounter with Jesus, became a brave, strong role model and notable asset to Jesus' team of disciples. At this point you may be thinking, if she is so wonderful and seemingly balanced, how does she relate to your 'out of control' theme? Be patient my friends, I am about to unravel Joanna's life to you in the way God showed me during a time I was wrestling with my own 'out of control' struggles.

Now, let me introduce you to this wonderful noble character, Joanna.

You will find this wonderful lady in just two scripture verses by name, and alluded references to her in others.

*Luke 8:1-3 (TLB): Not long afterwards he began a tour of the cities and villages of Galilee to announce the coming of the Kingdom of God, and took his twelve disciples with him. ²Some women went along, from whom he had cast out demons or whom he had healed; among them were Mary Magdalene (Jesus had cast out seven demons from her), ³**Joanna**, Chuza's wife (Chuza was King Herod's business manager and was in charge of his palace and domestic affairs), Susanna, and many others who were contributing from their private means to the support of Jesus and his disciples.*

*Luke 24:10 (TLB): The women who went to the tomb were Mary Magdalene and **Joanna** and Mary the mother of James, and several others.*

Firstly, from these two scriptures we find out four specific known things about Joanna's life.

The first thing we learn about her, is that she is the wife of Chuza, who is the financial manager of Herod's household. This meant that Joanna was a woman of great influence simply because she was married to a very powerful and influential man, Chuza. The second thing we find out about Joanna is that Jesus touched her and she was set free from an affliction. According to Luke 8:2, Joanna was either physically sick or had a demonic oppression on her life. The third known thing we read about her life is she was a financial supporter of Jesus. Being married to such a high-profile person as Chuza, she would have been a woman of great wealth and well able to support Jesus' ministry. And finally, we see that Joanna was one of the women who went to the tomb after Jesus' crucifixion to wash his body and there she met with an angel who told all who were there, including Joanna that He (Jesus) was no longer dead, but alive. This meant she was one of the very first to witness that Jesus had been resurrected, which is the very hope of our salvation.

What we don't read about Joanna or know of her life is quite intriguing.

We know nothing of her past. She is not mentioned once before being introduced in the scriptures we have just read. I have searched, believe me, and have came up with nothing. We don't know where she was born. We don't know what family bloodline Joanna came from, what village she grew up in, who her parents were or how many siblings she had. We don't know about her education level or what qualifications she had attained. We are not sure of her age or status before meeting her husband Chuza. We do not know how many children she had, or if she had any at all. We don't know what her religious beliefs were prior to her meeting Jesus. We don't even know what affliction she had or how it came upon her. So many unknowns and yet, here she is, popping up right in the middle of Jesus' ministry.

# 2
# REVEALING JOANNA

As I began to study Joanna's life, God spoke to me and said; 'Deb, I want you to look between the lines you are reading and as you do, listen to my voice. Listen to what I am going to teach you from her life'. As I began to ponder Joanna and her life, the Holy Spirit began to reveal to me some principles that helped me in my own journey towards wholeness.

What I learnt from her life between the lines...

Joanna's husband Chuza had a very prominent position being in charge of Herod's household and finances throughout the province of Galilee. He was one of the most influential, powerful and wealthiest men in Palestine. He no doubt lived in one of the finest homes in town and enjoyed the social prominence and status that came with his job. What that meant for Joanna was, she too experienced the privileges and luxurious lifestyle that came with being married to this man.

**In her position**, as the wife of Chuza, I could imagine that she could turn up to any restaurant and be given the best seat in the house. I envisage the waiters running around frantically as they see her approaching calling out to each other; 'Quickly, let's clear the best table, it's Chuza's wife'.

**In her position**, she knew that she could say to anyone under Chuza, do this or do that, and they would obey. She knew that if she needed anything, she simply had to say to one of Chuza's workers, please get me this or that and they would get it in an instant. This kind of control came by simply possessing the name Joanna, wife of Chuza.

**In her position**, Joanna possessed some power of control and as someone who had that kind of authority, she would be right to feel a certain amount of confidence about her life, knowing the influence and ability she had to make sure everything was right and good in her world.

Don't we all want that? To have the upper hand on life. The ability and assurance to make sure that everything is just as it should be in our own world. Ha ha…if only!

Luke 8:2 (TLB) says 'Soon afterward Jesus began a tour of the nearby towns and villages, preaching and announcing the Good News about the Kingdom of God. He took his twelve disciples with him, along with some women who had been cured of evil spirits and diseases (*Emphasis, mine*). Among them were Mary Magdalene, from whom he had cast out seven demons; Joanna, the wife of Chuza, Herod's business manager; Susanna; and many others'.

According to this scripture, we read that not everything was perfect in Joanna's world. She had an 'out of control' situation in her life that no amount of status, ability or influence she possessed, no amount of control, privilege or prominence she had, prevented her from being afflicted in some way. None of this helped when it came to getting what she needed most, being delivered, healed and set free.

We don't know if she had an evil spirit or some kind of disease, but whatever it was, it was serious, because all the money, influence and assistance available to her to receive the best of help was not working. Through Joanna's situation she found herself in a place of not being in control, but being out of control and not able to fix her own problem.

Sound familiar?

We don't know how long Joanna took in searching out self-help, it could have been weeks, months, even years, however at some stage in her search for solutions to her situation, she obviously came to the point of realizing she was not the answer to her 'out of control' issue.

How long does it take us to come to the point of realization that we are not the answer to situations that are out of our control or ability to do something about in the natural? Think about it for a moment. Be honest with yourself.

For me, until I took this personal journey of discovery and understanding that I don't have to be the 'saviour of my world', this was my lifestyle. You will learn more about my story in the next chapter.

We don't know how Joanna learned of Jesus, although I am sure His name was well known around town or at least becoming so. She was obviously curious enough about Jesus to seek Him out, when hearing He was going around town healing the sick. In the beginning she possibly thought he was just another doctor who could help her get some relief from the ailment she had. 'Maybe He can do something about my affliction'. Whether she knew of him as a simple healer, or even as the one whom He claimed to be - Jesus Christ, the Saviour of the world - it wasn't until she encountered Him personally, that she realised who He was in all His fullness and accepted all He could do for her.

She needed to come up close and personal with Him to recognise who He truly was. Not only did He heal her completely of her affliction, whether that be a physical or a spiritual one, He changed her life. She had known power and authority before, but now she was experiencing true power and authority. Jesus, You have my attention.

After her encounter with Jesus, she gained a bold trust. She put her faith in Him completely, even to the point of putting her own personal wealth behind His ministry, wealth that would have come through the hands of her husband, Chuza, Herod's business manager. Who knows what Chuza would have thought of this? She became one of Jesus' most devoted believers.

She openly followed Jesus and His disciples. As the wife of Chuza, who worked for Herod, it could have been dangerous for her, yet she chose to risk her reputation for the sake of the gospel. I don't believe she did this recklessly, I am sure she walked in wisdom; however, she didn't shrink back in fear either.

I call her brave because just maybe, she was the one who came to Jesus' rescue when He happened to just 'slip away' from those who tried to seize him. Luke 4:29-30 (CEV) and John 10:39 (MSG) speak of such times. Possibly Joanna had her own army of minders keeping an eye on Jesus, giving him room to get away.

Joanna was also mentioned as one of the few faithful followers who went to the tomb to find Jesus was not there after his resurrection. Luke 24:9-10 (NLT)

Before she met Jesus, she had a life that put her in a position of control over many things, except the one thing she needed most - healing of her infirmity. Placing that burden into the hands of the only one who could do something about it, opened up a whole new world for Joanna. It was the beginning of a bigger life for her. A ministry that would go down in biblical history. Her name was written in the word of God for a reason. Joanna did have her 'such a time as this' moment after all.

> It takes humility to know that all we possess in the natural, pales into insignificance compared to His almighty power.

When we are holding tightly onto situations, positions and even afflictions, that only Jesus can deal with, we waste precious time and energy. Releasing them into God's hands, not only gives Him room to move in our circumstances, but also allows Him to open up a bigger world for us to take hold of.

What I learnt from between the lines of Joanna's life, are in the key take away points listed below. I knew these things already, but knowing them as a rhema word is altogether different. You will find key take away nuggets after each and every story. Let these fundamental points be a measuring stick for where you see yourself and areas you need to face in order for you to gain a balanced life.

KEY TAKE AWAYS

- It takes an encounter with Jesus to know Him in His fullness.
- It takes getting up close and personal to learn that He will do for us what He says He will do.
- It takes action to trust Him with our lives.
- It takes willingness to surrender our control to realise His capability to hold all things in His hands.
- It takes humility to know that all we possess in the natural, pales into insignificance compared to His almighty power.
- It takes knowing Him, to realise His immeasurable love and heart towards us.
- It takes walking with Him to know He cares about our affliction, our circumstances, our 'out of control' situations more than we do.
- It takes making room for Him, to open up a bigger world to us.

**Part 2:** MY STORY

# 3
## BURDEN CARRIER

If you have read my book 'Just say YES', you would know that I was brought up in a dysfunctional home with a mentally ill father who was in and out of psychiatric hospitals all his married life, leaving my mother to be the sole care giver of her three children, my younger brother, my younger sister and me. Yes, that's right, I sit at the top of the chain, the eldest child.

It was a difficult life for my mother, yet she hardly ever complained and because my mother made our house a home and kept us safe, fed, and loved growing up, I never really understood just how tough it was for her and what a true hero she was until I got married and had children of my own.

I am fortunate and blessed to have married an amazing man who is a devoted partner in our life's journey, including bringing up our two children who are now grown and have children of their own. I thank God that my children grew up with both a mother *and* father, however, these days there are a lot of single parents out there doing it alone and I take my hat off, no, I applaud loud and long to those who are doing the sole parenting journey. I can't say I fully understand, but I have experienced seeing my mother do double duties without a break, not having that tag team relief and now also watching this same scenario with our daughter, who is bringing up four children on her own. I honour her resilience as she leads and guides those four precious grandies of ours.

Life can be lonely for the single parent who would just like to have a partner to turn to at any given moment to share the little things that have happened that day. Those who are single parents understand this, those who are not, take a moment to think of all the times that your partner is away or even just out for the day or evening and you find you are having to juggle the kids, the dinner, the homework and the mess all by yourself. For those of us who have a supportive partner, our saving grace is knowing it is but for a short period of time because help is on the way. It would be good for all of us to be a little more mindful of the single parent, not just in thought, but also in deed.

As a single parent, my mother, just like any other single parent, longed for someone to share her daily highs and lows with, but particularly those times when life would overwhelm her.

My father was sick. He had paranoid schizophrenia. Until I was in my teens, he would be in and out of psychiatric hospitals, which meant that when he was home, the atmosphere was tense. If he was heavily medicated, he was not a danger to us. However, when he would forget to take his tablets, not take them on time or at the correct dosage, he would become irrational and sometimes violent, and it was my mother who bore the brunt of that abuse. At his worst, he would become dangerously violent and during those times, he would be sent back to hospital where shock treatment was administered to settle him down.

We didn't have a landline phone at home, and in the 1970's there were no mobile phones either. There was no 'phone a friend' option for my mother, unless she went to a neighbour's home to use their phone and we only ever did that in emergencies. Although our grandmother was an amazing support to her and us three children, she wasn't always there during some of those times our mother needed someone to talk to, and it was then she would turn to me.

I remember her coming into my room, sometimes late at night and sharing with me things that were happening or how she was feeling. Being very young, I didn't know what to say, I had no answers, yet somehow, I felt I had to make my mother feel better.

I don't believe my mother ever meant to lay her burdens on me or expected me to remedy her situation, however the message I received in my spirit was, 'Help me feel better'. I thought I had to try and think of something to say to lift her spirit, to make her feel happy again, to somehow fix whatever situation or emotion she was going through at the time. Why I believed this to be my responsibility and felt so compelled to respond this way, I don't know. All I know is this, it began a pattern in me to be the 'fixer', the burden lifter, the peace keeper and the saviour of my world, lest it fall apart, and this pattern of behavior continued into my adulthood. It was my responsibility to be the super hero for the people in my life.

## THE SUPERGIRL STORY

Who is Supergirl? I am sure many of you know who she is because there have been movies and a television series made about her, however I cannot assume you all do.

For those who are not super hero fans, this wonder-girl came from a fictitious planet called Krypton, the same planet Superman came from. Many of you will be familiar with Superman, but did you know he had an older cousin who was none other than Supergirl?

Her baby cousin, Superman, had already been sent to earth because his parents wanted him to survive when their planet died. Supergirl's parents also wanted to send their daughter to earth, but for a different reason. She was being sent with a mission. The mission before her was this, 'Supergirl, go to earth and protect your baby cousin'.

However, on Supergirl's journey to earth things changed and she went off course putting her in a place where time stood still and she didn't age. When she arrived on earth, she was still thirteen, the age that she was when she left her planet. Now her cousin, Superman, was older than her. He had grown up. He was no longer in need of a protector as he had come into his own. He was mature, powerful and more than capable of looking after himself. Now Supergirl no longer had a mission, no longer had a purpose, so she decides to make the best of her life and just fit in.

This was all very well until she goes on her first blind date which didn't turn out that well. However, while still sitting at the bar where her date had dumped her, a newsflash comes on the television screen and she saw the very plane her sister, from her adoptive family on earth, was travelling on. She saw the plane wrapped in flames and heading for a crash landing. She could not just sit there, she had to do something. So, she did what any good sister would do. She changed into her super hero costume and flew up to the plane and rescued not only her sibling, but the whole plane. YAY, what a hero! And the rest is super hero history as they say. Supergirl went on to fight villians, stop trains, lift buses and everything else super heroes do in the many episodes of Supergirl that have been screened on television. She, being a super hero with super powers, had managed to save many a day.

Oh, to have a story like that. Unfortunately, none of us are super-human. I am not super-human, so I have discovered.

Supergirl on the other hand was. She always managed to succeed in making things right for those she helped, and it was never a burden to her. She would bounce back, full of energy and power, ready to take on the next impending disaster.

The truth is, Supergirl is a fictional character, a fantasy. She is not real. Her life does not depict what happens to real people in the real world.

# 4
## OUR FILTER SYSTEM

### REACTING THROUGH THE WRONG FILTER

I can't lift cars or buses. I can't fly or stop trains, but I can fight villains. The problem with some of my villain fighting scenarios, they were not mine to fight. I had given myself the title of rescuer from childhood, so in my mind, battles happening in my world *were* mine to combat.

I have discovered over the years though, that there is a difference between filling a need, offering advice or giving your opinion when asked for it, and being a control freak, the superhero who saves the day. A lot of my messes have come from the latter. The need to 'make it better', 'fix the problem at any cost', and take control, has definitely had its consequences. I may have saved the day, but more often than not, I would be left feeling exhausted and in a mess in pursuit of keeping the peace and creating a safe and secure zone for everyone else. I would often come away exhausted, overwhelmed with weariness from over trying. Some of my responses to situations did not always produce long term solutions to the problem anyway.

Control issues or any negative action for that matter, can often be played out because of the lenses we are looking through, and those lenses come from the experiences we ourselves have had. Here are two examples of reacting out of distorted vision.

I have a fabulous marriage. I feel incredibly blessed. Thank you, Paul, for being the best husband. However, due to the fact that my mother didn't have the same experience with my father that I did, I would feel guilty. When our daughter got married, I thought she was getting a husband like mine. He seemed perfect. Caring, attentive, considerate, just as you would expect a husband to be. Unfortunately, once they were married, things changed and the life we thought was to be equally as good as mine, was not. Whenever her then husband would treat her badly and she did not speak up, I would jump in and defend my daughter. I wanted her to be happy. I wanted fairness for my girl. That all sounds noble and the right thing to do, however, what I thought was saving her, was actually making it more difficult for her when I was not there. My actions to come to her aid came from a mixture of sadness for her and guilt that she didn't have what I have. Helping my daughter was right, however at times I would not ask my girl what she wanted before stepping in. I was coming to her defence through the filter of what I saw my mother grieve over, long for, and not have compared to what I, and others who have wonderful husbands have.

The other example comes from the fact that my father was a paranoid schizophrenic which was a result of his drug addiction. Seeing him at his worst, beating my mother, and in his nonsensical state, talking to himself both in the home and in public, greatly affected our family. I never knew my father in his pre-drug addiction days, but I was told he was kind, gentle, generous and a devoted husband and son. He deeply loved God and family. He had a brilliant mind, a photographic memory and breezed through school. I was told he went to high school when he was just ten years old because they couldn't hold him back. He went on to study to become a doctor but it was there that he had access to all kinds of drugs. He began experimenting with many of them which began to affect his mind. Six weeks before his final exams, he snapped. I saw on many occasions the fruit of what drugs did to him.

After a few years of us living in South East Asia where we serve God, our son decided to move back to Australia. He settled with family friends and he was doing well. Although we didn't contact him as much as we should have, we thought all was well in his world. Little did we know that he had begun hanging around with a different crowd of people who introduced him to drugs. We had no idea until he phoned us to tell us what was happening in his life. Our son came to the point where he knew he needed help. He took the brave step to ring us. He spent precious money to make the overseas call, got up the courage to reach out to us, his parents, and tell us that he was doing drugs and needed help. My response was not good. I got angry instead of listening. What our son was looking for from me was a listening ear, to be comforted, to hear he was still loved and valued and that we could work through this together. Unfortunately, my initial response gave him the opposite message. I was reacting out of the filter of what I experienced in my childhood with my father. I was reacting through the lense of my past.

Both of these reactions came out of seeing things through wrong lenses. The situations were very real and very true, but my responses to them were clouded by looking through the unfiltered lenses of my own past hurts and experiences, and my need to be in control. It is good and valuable to use the wisdom we have gained from our experience, however, there is a right way and a wrong way of doing this. The right way is being led by Godly wisdom. Listening to His wisdom and taking time to hear the voice of the Holy Spirit. Knowing when to speak, what to speak, and when to be silent; when to act, and when to hold your peace. Praying and trusting God to do what we cannot. This is where inner healing begins, *in us*.

## RESPONDING THROUGH GOD'S FILTER

Not every scenario was like these of course. In most situations I would listen to God's voice over my own. One particular circumstance comes to mind which I believe is a great example of how to do things in a healthy and balanced way, as opposed to the way that leaves a trail of pain and emotional turmoil, usually in the one who is trying take God's place in the situation by attempting to be in control.

Whenever we made major decisions as a family, we always included the kids in the decision making process because it was important that they too were on board with the plans we made. Our first big decision was our move from our home town of Newcastle in the state of New South Wales, Australia to the island state of Tasmania. It was the first of what were to be big moves that God would ask us to take as a family and you can read all about that in my first book, 'Just Say YES'.

Our second big move and call from God, came six years later when He called us from Tasmania, Australia to Vietnam. Again, we sat as a family to discuss this move and although more questions were raised from our kids now that they were older, it was a unanimous decision, this move was from God and we were all on board.

Before heading to Vietnam, we went back to our hometown of Newcastle to spend the final few weeks with family and friends. A new family had joined our old home church and on meeting them, we immediately clicked and were invited back to their home for lunch. It was here that our son met their daughter and need I say more, all of a sudden, that God call to the mission field didn't matter anymore. 'Mum, I don't want to go to Vietnam, I want to stay here'. Well of course, at fifteen years of age, that wasn't going to happen, and although he and this new girl in his life were not happy about it, he came with us to Vietnam. They kept in contact but after a year or so, he was back in Australia where he and his then girlfriend were able to have a face to face relationship.

At first things were ok between them, but as time went on the relationship turned toxic. It wasn't that this girl was bad or that our son was bad, but together, they brought out the worst in each other and our boy was moving further and further away from his first love, Jesus. He was not doing well and often shared with Paul and I situations that were happening in the relationship which were tearing him apart, yet at the same time, he would repeatedly tell us that he didn't want to break up with her and he definitely didn't want us to say anything against the relationship. It was during those times, I would feel helpless and frustrated that I could not 'fix it' for him or rescue him. By now, he was eighteen and of an age where he could make his own decisions and being eighteen, really wasn't wanting to listen to us, so we turned to God as our only answer. They were together for three years, and for three years my husband and I prayed. Paul could pray, leave it with God and sleep at night. Me, on the other hand, would pray, then pray some more and then stew over the situation. I would pray into the night and early hours of the morning until I fell asleep. There is nothing wrong with praying, even into the early hours of the morning if God has you doing this, but I had allowed this situation to consume me.

One night after a distressing phone call from our son, I crawled into bed in anguish, crying out to God, 'What do I do, what do I do?' I remember drifting off to sleep around midnight or a little later, but found myself awake again with the heaviness on my heart for our son and this relationship that was destroying him. I again cried out to God, 'God, I can't be in South East Asia helping people here, working to restore lives here, while my son is going downhill fast, I need to go back to Australia and help my son'. In my mind I began to make plans on how I was going to help our son. How *I* was going to 'help him'. How I was going to make it right with his world, but in the midst of the planning, I was wise enough to know that I needed a 'God solution' more.

After I prayed that prayer to God, the Holy Spirit spoke very clearly to me and He said, 'Deb, if you go back now, you will only do a 'band aid' job. Leave him to me. Your job is to pray for him'. I knew that had to be the Holy Spirit speaking to me because my mother's heart was wanting to do the opposite - run to save my son.

There is nothing that equals the voice of the Holy Spirit speaking directly into your spirit. As soon as He said that, a peace came upon me and for the first time since praying for this relationship, I knew I could leave this in God's hands even though I didn't know how God was going to handle it.

That prayer was said in the September and three months later, in the December, we were to have our son and his girlfriend come for Christmas. We were so excited to see him but we were concerned about the visit. Although God had spoken to me and said, 'Leave it to me', I still felt a little anxious. Despite how I felt, I knew God was going to do something. My hope in His ability to do what He promised was greater than my fear that nothing would change.

December came and just weeks out from our son and his girlfriend arriving, we got a phone call from him to say he had been offered some work which would take him right up to Christmas time and would it be ok to come after Christmas. He then went on to say that he would be coming alone because his girlfriend couldn't come after Christmas. Already God was at work.

Before our son arrived, God spoke to me again and said, 'I don't want you to say anything about the relationship, just love him. Let me do the work'. He came for two weeks and for the first week we just enjoyed being together, being a family. I kept my promise and said nothing about the relationship but at night when he went to bed, Paul and I would pray. On the Monday evening of the second week, we all went to bed as usual, but at 1am there was a knock on our bedroom door. It was our son. He said, 'Can I come in and chat to you? God has just spoken to me and told me I need to break up with my girlfriend, come back under your covering and get right with God again'.

I was speechless, literally. What we had been praying for, for over three years, we were now seeing God do. Needless to say, none of us slept the rest of that night. We sat and talked, cried and prayed. Returning to break the news to his girlfriend was not going to be an easy task. I told him, 'Get a word from God, a promise from Him which will hold you and sustain you, because the enemy doesn't want you to turn your heart back to God'. Over the next week he spent time with God and every scripture he read had the word 'rescue' in it. 'I've come to rescue you'. 'I will rescue you'. God did something deep in his heart that Monday night and during the rest of the week, something I could never have done. God did it.

Towards the end of the second week as our son was preparing to go back to Australia in order to finish up at his workplace, pack up his belongings and do the most difficult thing, break the news to his girlfriend, God spoke to me again and said, 'Deb, now you can go. Go support your son and do whatever he needs you to do. Be his prayer warrior, be an ear for him to debrief to. Be a mum for him'.

Hearing the whisper of the Holy Spirit among the turmoil and obeying that voice will make all the difference. Listening to His voice in the midst of the noise of a situation that is shouting loud at you for attention, will calm your storm and give you a better perspective. When our son first rang to tell us how bad things were between him and his girlfriend, all I wanted to do was to make it better, to fix it, but because it was an 'out of control' situation I had no answers. Thank God I was desperate enough to pray and listen. Not pray and then take the reins.

Today this son of ours is a pastor, a husband of an amazing wife, and a father to three of our beautiful grandbabies. He loves God and loves people. Everyone who meets him, sees God all over him.

I had learnt a great lesson from this situation with our son. I learnt just how incredible God is at doing a lasting work in someone that we could never do ourselves. The Holy Spirit is the greatest of surgeons and He can get into places in our hearts where man can never reach.

God can do more than we ask or imagine in ways we stand amazed at. Allow yourself to be astounded by what can happen when we let go and allow God to take the reins.

> Allow yourself to be astounded by what can happen when we let go and allow God to take the reins.

*'For all the promises of God in Him are Yes, and in Him Amen, to the glory of God through us.'* 2 Corinthians 1:20 (NKJV)

When God says 'yes' He means, unquestionable. My promises are unquestionable. God's 'amen' translates as 'let it be so'. What God is saying in 2 Corinthians 1:20 is 'Let what I have declared be known as unquestionable and that it will come to pass'.

# 5
## LESSONS LEARNT BUT EASILY FORGOTTEN

When you have a habit that has been in your life for a long time, it can take a while to break that habit. It is not that you are necessarily a bad student of God, it can simply be because you do what comes natural to you when things seemingly are about to go wrong.

Who of you, when putting your complete trust in the immeasurable work of God, have seen Him do incredible miracles, change situations and move hearts in your own world? I am sure you can think of many examples, situations or occasions.

Who of you though, have found yourselves defaulting back to, 'Will God come through?' the next time a difficult situation arises? I know I have. I could go from one day to the next, from: 'God you are faithful, I am standing strong in my belief for you to come through,' to 'Oh God, I am fearful, where is your power?' I am so thankful that I am not such a yoyo these days because I have seen God's incredible hand on each and every situation that has come my way, and I have learnt to draw on His past faithfulness.

I am not saying I have mastered the art of letting go, however I am much more aware of when my tendencies lean towards the old habits of the past. I have definitely moved closer to fully trusting God every day, not just when I 'feel' God is near or 'feel' sure of His faithfulness.

One of the best examples of being guilty of yoyo faith in the Bible, is found in the book of 1 Kings, chapter 18.

In this chapter, we read the account of a man named Elijah. He is remembered as the servant of God who stood boldly before his enemy Ahab, challenging him and his 400 prophets of their god Baal, to a test - test to prove whose god was the true God. Their idol god Baal, or Elijah's true and living God.

[21] *Elijah went before the people and said, 'How long will you waver between two opinions? If the Lord is God, follow him; but if Baal is God, follow him'.*

The people remained noncommittal at that point. Elijah then challenged his enemies to build an altar to their god, to collect wood for the altar, kill a bull, cut it up and place it on the altar. Elijah said he would do the same. He then went on to say, that they were not to light a fire on their altar but call on their god to bring the fire. The God who came through would be considered the true God. The prophets of Baal agreed that it was a good plan so they did what Elijah asked and then they began to call out to their god to send down fire.

When Elijah put out this challenge to his enemies, he spoke with confidence, determination and unwavering faith. He was sure his God would not let him down.

[23] *'Get two bulls for us. Let Baal's prophets choose one for themselves, and let them cut it into pieces and put it on the wood but not set fire to it. I will prepare the other bull and put it on the wood but not set fire to it.* [24] *Then you call on the name of your god, and I will call on the name of the Lord. The god who answers by fire – he is God'. Then all the people said, 'What you say is good'.* [25] *Elijah*

said to the prophets of Baal, 'Choose one of the bulls and prepare it first, since there are so many of you. Call on the name of your god, but do not light the fire'. [26] So they took the bull given them and prepared it. Then they called on the name of Baal from morning till noon. 'Baal, answer us!' they shouted. But there was no response; no one answered. And they danced around the altar they had made.[27] At noon Elijah began to taunt them. 'Shout louder!' he said. 'Surely he is a god! Perhaps he is deep in thought, or busy, or traveling. Maybe he is sleeping and must be awakened'.

You can imagine Elijah having a great time watching and taunting these guys as they did crazy things to get the attention of their so-called god. Doing crazy things to get Baal to answer them, but the more these prophets of Baal called out to their god, the more frustrated they became.

[28] So they shouted louder and slashed themselves with swords and spears, as was their custom, until their blood flowed. [29] Midday passed, and they continued their frantic prophesying until the time for the evening sacrifice. But there was no response, no one answered, no one paid attention.

Then it was Elijah's turn. He was calm, cool and collected as he began building his altar to the living God. In fact, he was so sure God would turn up, he asked the people to gather around, making sure that all eyes were on him and ready to see what God was about to do. In other words, Elijah was saying, 'Well now that you have tired yourselves out trying to get the attention of *your* god, check out just how alive and true *my* God is'. Then just to prove a point, Elijah went one step further to show that nothing was impossible with the creator of the universe by completely saturating the altar with water.

[30] Then Elijah said to all the people, 'Come here to me'. They came to him, and he repaired the altar of the Lord, which had been torn down. [31] Elijah took twelve stones, one for each of the tribes descended from Jacob, to whom the word of the Lord had come, saying, 'Your name shall be Israel'. [32] With the stones he built an altar in the name of the Lord, and he dug a trench around it large enough to hold two seahs of seed. [33] He arranged the wood, cut the bull into pieces and laid it on the wood. Then he said to them, 'Fill four large jars with water and pour it on the offering and on the wood'. [34] 'Do it again', he said, and they did it again.

*'Do it a third time', he ordered, and they did it the third time. ³⁵ The water ran down around the altar and even filled the trench. ³⁶ At the time of sacrifice, the prophet Elijah stepped forward and prayed: 'Lord, the God of Abraham, Isaac and Israel, let it be known today that you are God in Israel and that I am your servant and have done all these things at your command. ³⁷ Answer me, Lord, answer me, so these people will know that you, Lord, are God, and that you are turning their hearts back again'.*

Then God did what Baal could never do.

*³⁸ Then the fire of the Lord fell and burned up the sacrifice, the wood, the stones and the soil, and also licked up the water in the trench. ³⁹ When all the people saw this, they fell prostrate and cried, 'The Lord – he is God! The Lord – he is God!'*

And in true God form, He went above and beyond, not only lighting the fire to burn the sacrifice, but also the wood, the stones, the soil and every drop of water. God demonstrated His miracle working power. What a God we serve and good on you Elijah for having the faith to believe your prayers would be answered. What a faith filled man you are. What a brave soul, going against so many of your enemies like that. High five Elijah. Going forward, you can believe for anything now, right? Wrong!

In 1 Kings 19:1-5 we read that it was not long before Elijah forgot the incredible victory he had experienced; the miracle God did for him just days ago. How quickly his faith flew out the window, and fear took its place when another situation came against him causing him to say, 'I am out of here, this is too much'.

*¹Now Ahab told Jezebel everything Elijah had done and how Elijah had killed all the prophets with a sword. ² So Jezebel sent a messenger to Elijah, saying, 'May the gods punish me terribly if by this time tomorrow I don't kill you just as you killed those prophets'. ³ When Elijah heard this, he was afraid and ran for his life, taking his servant with him. When they came to Beersheba in Judah, Elijah left his servant there. ⁴ Then Elijah walked for a whole day into the desert. He sat down under a bush and asked to die. 'I have had enough, Lord', he prayed. 'Let me die. I am no better than my ancestors'. ⁵ Then he lay down under the tree and slept.*

Sound familiar to anyone? I am sure you know exactly what I am talking about here, right? Come on, be honest. The stories I have shared with you so far from my life are not much different to Elijah, and I am sure not much different to yours either. How do I know this? You picked up this book and looked at the title and thought; 'Out of control', 'hmmm, sometimes I feel out of control'. I am smiling at you here my friend, because I get you.

# 6
## THE STRAW THAT BROKE THE CAMEL'S BACK.

For those of you who do not know me: my family and I are missionaries who have and continue to serve in a closed country that is full of restrictions and often filled with frustration and loads of red tape. Yet, it has not been those things, or the country we serve in, that have caused me to have 'out of control' moments, as difficult as it has been at times. I have not had the intense urge to control situations in our field of service. The battleground within me has been much closer to home.

You will remember I previously mentioned that I felt it was my responsibility to make things better, to make things right, for my mother in my younger years and that the pattern for this perceived responsibility continued into my adult years. The 'straw that broke the camel's back', so to speak, came in 2014. The mindset which had taken up residence in my thinking was about to be challenged by God himself after four 'out of control' situations were thrust upon me and my family, one after the other within a year.

Over twenty years ago, my mother re-married and when she married, I was so happy for her. I was happy to see that she now had a partner to share life with and to know my mother was not lonely any more. I was incredibly happy that she had found a life partner and it was also a relief to me that the burden of her being on her own was now lifted from my shoulders. I am not saying we should not care for our parents or look out for their needs, but my issue of feeling guilt or the need to rush in and fix things for her was not necessarily the best way to show it. Seeing how happy and content she was now, even though she was getting on in years and had health problems, was comforting to me.

All this changed however, when in 2014 my step-father was diagnosed with cancer and passed away within months. Now my mother was once again on her own and alone.

I am blessed to have a sister who, because she lives in our hometown and close to our mum, cared for her well. Thank you, sis. She looked out for mum's needs before, during and after the death of my step-father. However, for me, that default characteristic in me came rushing to the forefront. 'I have to fix this'. But this was not a fixable situation. I could not do anything about what had just happened. I could not bring her husband back, nor could I fix my mother's heartbreak. I did what any daughter would do and I was there for her, but this crazy nagging feeling of 'how can I make it better for her' was tormenting me. I allowed it to become a heavy burden that I carried internally.

For many years my sister did not have a life partner herself, so at times she felt quite lonely. When we got the news that she had finally met someone, this was music to my ears. Another family member happy. He was to be her partner for life, however after being together for fourteen years, and just nine months after our step-father passed away, my sister's partner died suddenly and without warning. Now she was alone and heartbroken also. 'How can I fix this? How can I make this one better?' I could not. Another perceived responsibility I believed was in my hands to rectify was now dropping like juggling balls slipping out of my grip.

Four weeks later, my daughter rang Paul and I from Australia. She wanted her husband to reveal to us the many things that he had been doing to cause even further strife to our girl. He came on the phone and he told us in a light hearted, 'it will be alright', manner, what he had done, but the message was clear. The situation he had put her in was about to send her down the road of bankruptcy, leaving her with a bad name. Not only that, it could have also put her in potential physical danger, due to the manner in which he had done business. There had always been issues in the marriage, but the problems he had caused this time were the final straw. The ache in my heart was immense and my first reaction was, once again, 'I have to fix this one!' The third proverbial ball had fallen out of my hands. It was something else I could not mend.

The icing on the cake came just two months later when my mother got sick and she too was diagnosed with cancer. My first thought was, 'Oh God no, not this too!'

It was at this point I went into a downward spiral. I cried out to God. 'All these things God, and I can't fix one of them!' Although I cried out to God, desperately wanting to hear from him, I couldn't hear Him speak. I was allowing my own thoughts to shout louder. My focus was on how I could make all these situations better in my family's world.

At this point I am sure there are some of you reading this thinking, 'She is reading my life!'

Yes, I know. When I was sharing with friends and others the outline of this book, some would be quick to respond with, 'Oh, I need this book'. Too many of us find ourselves in a place of feeling the responsibility to fix situations we don't have the ability to fix, and have not been asked to 'resolve', yet we just can't help ourselves by jumping in to save the day like Supergirl. We feel the need to be the answer, the 'God' for others' lives in order for everyone and everything to be right in their world and in turn, see our own world be at peace again.

After these four significant events happened, I found myself not even coping well with the day to day responsibilities I actually did have in my life. The things I was usually on top of and loved to do now felt burdensome. I don't know when it started, but I soon found myself playing a mindless game on my phone, something I was not in the habit of doing as I am not a video games type of person. The game itself was harmless, but it become an escape for me to not have to think of the situations that were in my life that were out of my control. My thinking at the time subconsciously was, 'If I can't fix these situations, I don't want to feel at all'.

I found myself playing this mindless game throughout the day and sometimes up to two hours at a time. After I would finish playing a game, I would then become angry with myself for playing such a mindless game because it didn't achieve anything and it didn't change anything. As a task orientated person in particular, I would be disappointed in myself for wasting so much time and yet I would return to it day after day to escape the pain of the burdens that were totally out of my ability to do anything about. Crazy, ay?

A few months passed and nothing had changed in my personal life. I was still in this cycle of crying out to God for help for the situations, trying to hear from Him then closing down again and playing the mindless game that had become my escape place. I had let circumstances out of my control consume me, rather than release them completely to the only one who could do anything about it. I would hand them over at the altar, then pick them back up again before I left God's presence.

My husband, although very encouraging and supportive of me, didn't know how to help me through this because his thinking is so different. He is so stable, so centered and looks at things in a balanced healthy way. He prays and then trusts God to come through. You would think this would be enough for me, right?

After months of allowing myself to get to this point, I received a life line - a good friend of ours came to visit. Even though I was in this crazy cycle, God was still listening and He was working behind the scenes. This friend was not only a pastor, but a trained counsellor. He took one look at me and said, 'Deb, what's wrong with you?' My reply,

'I'm fine!' His response, 'No you're not. What's going on in your life?' My reply once again, 'I'm fine'. Then it all came out like a flood. His diagnosis, 'Deb, you are at rock bottom, so right now you have to stop doing everything, take time out from your ministry and get well or you will have a breakdown'. He gave me a few keys, but the greatest tool for healing came after our friend left. It came from God himself.

## I'M FINE

How many of us, particularly those of us in ministry, feel we have to respond with 'I'm fine' as a public face, when we are at times, clearly not? We have this false belief that because we are leaders, mentors, well known or relied upon, we cannot be known or seen to have difficult times, whether that be feeling like we are in a position that is beyond our depth, experiencing emotional pressure greater than what we are capable of handling or becoming too busy. We might feel the need to get off the merry-go-round for a moment to take a breath, but believe we can't. We want everyone to believe we have it all together, that we are strong and we can handle whatever comes our way. This is a tactic of the enemy.

The enemy's strategy is to see us burn out. He whispers in our ear, 'Keep going, keep going, keep the smile up, keep doing more good things, godly things even, don't tell anyone you need someone to help you because that will make you look weak'.

I am not advocating that you shout it from the rooftops, but you need to recognize the signs and you must, when you need to, share with a trustworthy friend, mentor, counsellor or pastor before you break. It does not make you weak. It does not make you incapable of what God created you for. You simply need someone to come and lift up your hands for a while and walk with you through the tough times.

Even Moses needed his hands lifted up when he got tired. When the Amalekites came to attack the Israelites, Moses sent men to go and fight against them. Moses however, said I will stand at the top of the hill with the staff of God and raise my hands.

*¹⁰ So Joshua fought the Amalekites as Moses had ordered, and Moses, Aaron and Hur went to the top of the hill. ¹¹ As long as Moses held up his hands, the Israelites were winning, but whenever he lowered his hands, the Amalekites were winning. ¹² When Moses' hands grew tired, they took a stone and put it under him and he sat on it. Aaron and Hur held his hands up – one on one side, one on the other – so that his hands remained steady till sunset. ¹³ So Joshua overcame the Amalekite army with the sword. ¹⁴ Then the Lord said to Moses, 'Write this on a scroll as something to be remembered and make sure that Joshua hears it, because I will completely blot out the name of Amalek from under heaven'. ¹⁵ Moses built an altar and called it; The Lord is my Banner. ¹⁶ He said, 'Because hands were lifted up against the throne of the Lord, the Lord will be at war against the Amalekites from generation to generation'. Exodus17:10-16*

<u>Two key points here.</u> Firstly, Moses was still the leader. There is no question about that. He did however, come to the point where he realised he needed assistance. It is here we see that Moses was mature enough to allow trusted people to come alongside him and hold up his hands when the weight of responsibility became too much for him. Moses didn't say, 'No I can do it myself'. He didn't say, 'What will people think when they see me get help through this period?' He allowed others to bear the weight with him until the battle was won. Secondly, no one said to Moses, 'It's obvious that you can't do your job, we need to remove you from your post'. Those who stood by him, helped him through it, not hurled him out.

If you are feeling the weight of a situation that could overwhelm you, don't wait to ask for someone to come and hold your hands up for a while.

# 7
## WISING UP

I stayed at home, resting as prescribed and our pastor-counsellor friend checked in on me a couple of times a week, even after he returned to his home. He continued to make sure I was doing OK and not doing anything I felt I could not handle during that time. What a godsend. I did what I was told; stayed at home, tried to read the word of God and I prayed. The only other thing I did was, you guessed it, play that mindless game that kept me from thinking about anything that would pull me towards my unhealthy 'control' actions.

Several days had passed since my orders were given, 'Stay home, let go of responsibilities, and get well', and each day I did my best to do what I was told to do. I would get up, pray and tell God that I would try harder. I read the word and tried to not waiver from trusting God to heal my own thought processes and help my family.

The problem was, my dysfunctional concept of believing that I needed to fix things would inevitably return because I was still trying to help myself. 'I' being the operative word. I wasn't getting it. I still thought I was the 'fixer' and now I was trying to fix myself. This is where each of us can come undone if we don't deal with broken places in our lives. Broken people can't fix broken people. Only our creator, the perfect one, can heal, revive, restore and renew us by the power of the Holy Spirit. This is the healthy, fruitful and more permanent option.

> *'Heal me, O Lord, and I shall be healed; save me, and I shall be saved; for you are my praise'. Jeremiah 17:14 (NKJV)*

The healthy pathway is to pray, commit our needs, our plans, our worries to God, and then choose to believe that God is working on our behalf in all of the things we cannot fix or change. We have to make the decision to stand firm in our belief in God's ability, even if the road seemingly becomes rockier at first. Jesus is the true restorer of our soul and the One who holds the key to every situation.

The unhealthy, dysfunctional road can sound very similar. Pray, commit our needs, our plans, our worries to God, then we *hope* He is on the case. We muster up a, 'fingers crossed' kind of trust, but the cloud of doubt muddies our faith. We end up going forward, not faith based, but fear based. We enter God's throne room with our concerns, handing each one over to Him, telling God we trust Him and His ability to answer our needs, but the moment we turn to exit the sanctuary, we snatch those troubles back off Him again, returning them to our backpack, and struggle out the door, bent over from the heavy burden we came in with. We then wonder why nothing has changed. For some of us, that taking back is immediate, for others it can be a gradual thing. The point is, we maintain the urge to regain control lest everything falls apart. Whether it be consciously or subconsciously, our default rationale says, 'I must handle it because it may not be done in time or the way I want to see it unfold'.

If you are still reading this book, it says to me you are looking for answers to the cycle of control that has you collapsing under the weight of unrealistic burdens that you carry. We all struggle to a degree with control. Again, whether consciously or unconsciously, we all have an area we find difficult to hand over. 'God, I trust you completely with my finance, but I don't know if I can trust you with my future. Lord I trust you with my health, but I find it hard to trust you with my family'. Sound familiar? For some of us it's just one or two areas, for others it's everything. For me it was the need to make everything right, happy and balanced in my family's world and those around me. Sounds fair enough, but not when you don't give room for God to move or breathing space for others to grow themselves.

Thank God that He loves us too much to leave us in this unhealthy state. That is why He sent Jesus to set us free.

> *'It is for freedom that Christ has set us free. Stand firm, then, and do not let yourselves be burdened again by a yoke of slavery'. Galatians 5:1*

He has come to give us life and life to the full. For freedom, He has set us free. Not just one or two of us, but all of us. Not just for one or two areas in our lives, but for every area in our life. Galatians 5:1 says, 'Let's not be burdened again'. In other words, Let's not be ones who have to learn our lesson a second, a third, or a hundredth time. Don't continue in the habit of putting the unnecessary burden on yourself over and over again. He comes along side of us, waiting for us to be still and hear His whisper, to hear His Spirit of truth say, 'Be free. It is for freedom, that Christ has set us free'.

## GOD'S WHISPER

Being obedient to the counsel of our pastor friend I stayed at home, prayed and worked on getting well. I was so frustrated with myself for getting to this point. One day, as I was contemplating where I was at, yearning to hear from God, just sitting still, I began to sense the presence of the Holy Spirit in the room. His presence became so tangible I could almost touch it. He began to speak and His voice was crystal clear. He spoke to me, not in a judgmental way, but in a soft loving way. He said, 'Deb, what are you doing? You are better than this and you know Me better than this. Who told you that you are the burden carrier? When did I ever lay that on you? Jesus is your burden carrier. In fact, that is His portfolio and you have taken His portfolio from Him. Jesus is asking you to hand it back to Him. While you hold it, He cannot do anything. It is only when you give back to Him what is His, that He can truly work on your behalf'.

Pause and listen again to what the Holy Spirit said to me: *'Who told you that you are the burden carrier? When did I ever lay that on you? Jesus is your burden carrier. In fact, that is His portfolio and you have taken His portfolio from Him. Jesus is asking you to hand it back to Him. While you hold it, He cannot do anything. It is only when you give back to Him what is His, that He can truly work on your behalf'.*

Wow - Jesus' portfolio! I had never thought of it that way before. One of Jesus' job descriptions, one of His 'portfolios', is 'burden carrier'. Jesus carries many significant names, has many 'portfolios' and burden carrier is one of these. It is His responsibility. I had read those words many times and I even knew it, believed it and preached about it, but now it was a revelation to my own soul. It hit my spirit like a ton of bricks as I saw myself going into Jesus' heavenly 'office' and taking His 'Burden Carrier' portfolio off His bookshelf and carrying it out. What a ridiculous scenario. We can all be guilty of doing that from time to time, right?

The key to moving forward is believing by faith the truth that it is not by our feelings, but by choosing to trust, despite our feelings. Either His word, His whole word, is truth, or it's not. The enemy's portfolio is to put doubts into our mind, to kill, steal and destroy. He will try and steal our joy, our peace, our trust, and put things on us that we were never meant to carry.

> *'Praise be to the Lord, to God our Saviour, who daily bears our burdens. Our God is a God who saves; from the Sovereign Lord comes escape from death'.*
> Psalm 68:19-20

So, should we carry burdens at all? Yes. We all have responsibilities that we must not neglect. However, Jesus promises us, that the burdens given to us are not heavy weighted, crushing our soul, but are easy to bear, light to carry.

> *Then Jesus said, 'Come to me, all of you who are weary and carry heavy burdens, and I will give you rest. <sup>29</sup>Take my yoke upon you. Let me teach you, because I am humble and gentle at heart, and you will find rest for your souls.<sup>30</sup> For my yoke is easy to bear, and the burden I give you is light'.*
> Matthew 11:28-30 (NLT)

When this revelation came to me from the Holy Spirit that day, without hesitation I immediately deleted the game I was playing from my computer and my phone. For me, it was like a chain had fallen off me. That is the power of God speaking His word straight into our spirit. God's word has the power to shift our thinking from one direction to another.

The initial revelation to my spirit was electric but the process to wholeness took time. We need to understand this point. It is very rare that habits fall off us instantaneously. I have heard testimonies of this happening and God bless those who have this experience, however, for the majority of us, it is a process. It is a step by step, day by day, and sometimes hour by hour exercise. Don't beat yourself up about it if change doesn't come as quickly as it does for other people you may know of or you have read about.

After my initial response of listening and receiving His gentle but firm command to me and deleting my 'escape from reality' game, I asked God, 'Now what? How do I get better? How do I overcome this life-long need to control each situation? What do I do? How can I do it?'

Questions, questions, questions. I, I, I. Isn't it good that God is a long-suffering Father? I am sure He was waiting for me to finish babbling on so He could continue what He had begun sharing with me. He said, 'Deb, I am not asking YOU to do the restoration work alone. Allow ME to do this with you'.

We need to recognise that we are made up of body, soul and spirit. Therefore, to be truly whole, our whole being needs to healthy. We need to understand that each part is connected to the other. We cannot say, 'My body is healthy, I look after it, I eat well, discipline myself and get enough sleep', yet all the while suffer with a broken spirit. It's like functioning on two or three of the cylinders in your four-cylinder car. To regain a healthy life, you need a healthy body, a healthy soul, and a healthy spirit, and with everything in balance, you gain a healthy balanced controlled life.

God began to give me strategies to put into place in order to recover and gain a new mindset. He put tools in my hands that began to renew my mind and restore my soul.

## LAUGHTER

The first tool He gave me was laughter. He said to me, 'Deb, you need to laugh again'. I thought it was interesting that laughter was the first tool He gave me. To laugh! I thought I did laugh. According to the word of God, laughter is vital medicine for our soul.

> *'A happy heart is good medicine and* a joyful mind causes healing, *but a broken spirit dries up the bones'. Proverbs 17:22 (AMP)*

I needed to laugh again. I mean really laugh. It wasn't that I didn't laugh, I did. I laughed often, however the knot inside me did not afford me the freedom to completely let go. The stress and tension of trying to juggle all the balls of life that I felt were my responsibility to fix, and which I believed had been thrown my way but were now dropping or more like smashing, caused any laughter I expressed to stay at surface level. It did not get down into my belly, my soul, where it could do me good. I began to listen to good clean comedians who made me laugh hard and I felt the effects of this laughter immediately.

According to Doctor Jeanne Segal, Ph.D and her team of experienced medical practitioners, laughter has many healing properties. As reported in an article on Doctor Segal's website, helpguide.org, under the subject 'Laughter is the best medicine', laughter can restore our health on many levels.

This report tells us that laughter strengthens your immune system, boosts mood, diminishes pain, and protects you from the damaging effects of stress. Nothing works faster or more dependably to bring your mind and body back into balance than a good laugh. Humour lightens your burdens, inspires hope, connects you to others, and keeps you grounded, focused, and alert. It also helps you release anger and makes forgiveness easier.

To learn more about the benefits of laughter, you can find the link in the back of this book under references.

## SPIRITUAL FOOD

The second tool God gave me was to learn the art of being still and staying silent. This tool would give God space to speak deep into my spirit. To give time for His word to soak in. Be still. Be silent. Let God do the talking. To be still and to be silent takes discipline. We have to get ourselves out of the way.

> *'My child, pay attention to what I say. Listen carefully to my words.*
> [21] *Don't lose sight of them. Let them penetrate deep into your heart,*
> [22] *for they bring life to those who find them, and healing to their whole body'.*
> *Proverbs 4:20-22 (NLT)*

This takes discipline and it takes preparation. Intentionally organising the time and the place that works for you to become still and silent. I found 'my space', and I would go there, listen to worship music for a few moments and then become silent in His presence. I let His word penetrate my thinking and soak into my soul. I chose scriptures to meditate on that spoke of God's immeasurable love, goodness and ability. I would quote those verses continually, until they became part of my inner being. Scriptures like I have mentioned already.

For my daughter's situation, I sought God for a word that would be a promise to see her come through the other side. He gave me Exodus 14. A word that would see her cross the seas on dry land and all her enemies would be drowned while coming after her. The perfect rhema word. You can't get a word like that when you are too busy talking or wrapped up in trying to be the answer to a situation that only God has solutions for.

Only when we become still and silent, allowing God room to speak, do we hear from Him clearly. I knew this word was God's promise to my girl and He was saying to me, 'I've got this'. There is power in the listening. A word from God that speaks directly into your spirit, is an anchor to your soul. It becomes an 'I know that I know' word, and in that same moment, an exchange takes place. Exchange of worry for faith. Whenever the storm rose up, Paul and I would go to that word and speak it out and into the situation. I could look at that passage of scripture, pray over it and leave it. I made the choice to believe what it said. Sometimes things seemingly got worse after I prayed, but I kept quoting that passage, beginning with, 'God you said'. I would also tell him how I felt. It is ok to be honest about how you feel because He knows anyway. 'God, I feel worried, however, I choose to believe your word instead of worrying'.

> 'So shall My word be that goes forth from My mouth;
> It shall not return to Me void, But it shall accomplish what I please,
> And it shall prosper in the thing for which I sent it'.
> Isaiah 55:11 (NKJV)

## TRUSTED AARONS AND HURS

The third tool God gave me was Aarons and Hurs. God told me, this is not something the world needs to know, but share with trusted people who will encourage you and hold your hands up through the process just as Aaron and Hur did for Moses.

What do Aarons and Hurs look like? You will recognise them as people in your life who want to see you thrive and see you become all you are called to be. They don't deplete you; they fuel you. They respect you, are loyal to you and are trustworthy. They will be honest with you but will not judge you. They will love you unconditionally. The bottom line is, we cannot be prideful, thinking we don't need help when we go through challenging seasons. In fact, the most mature thing we can do is confide in our Aarons and Hurs. Moses knew he could trust in Aaron and Hur. He knew that they would be the ones to stay by his side until the battle was conquered. Aaron and Hur took an arm each. Both of them played a specific role in helping Moses, each with their own ability. Choose wisely your Aarons and Hurs.

Now I am able to share my story with the whole world. I can do that *now*. In fact, I needed to share with you so you can glean from my story what God has taught me.

KEY TAKE AWAYS

- You are not defined by your past. 2 Corinthians 5:17
- If you have a black belt in control like I did, ask yourself at what point the need to control began.
- None of us are perfect. Being imperfect does not disqualify you as a useful or worthwhile person or exclude you from your calling.
- 'Burden Carrier' is Jesus' portfolio, not yours. Psalm 68:19-20
- Being in control is different to being responsible.
- Trust in the Lord with all your heart. All. The same way you have trust for one area of life, learn to trust Him the same way in the areas you feel you need to control. Proverbs 3:5-6
- Be still and know that I am God. Psalm 46:10
- Find your Aarons and Hurs.

# Part 3: THEIR STORY

# 8
## YOU ARE NOT ALONE

Have you sat and analysed why you feel the need to control? What is the trigger point?

What has sparked the need to react and defend yourself or others in a strong way? Who has told you that you need to be the one to jump in, that you are the only one who can save the day, lest the world cave in if you don't? Don't get me wrong, I know your intentions are good. I believe they come from a place of true love, usually a sacrificial love on your part. You want to do your best to save others pain and heartache, that is your motivation right? However, not all intentions that are good equate to fruitfulness, or are helpful long-term solutions.

Maybe your form of control is the one that causes you to default to self-protection mode. Always working hard to have all your ducks lined up in a row, everything perfect, or at least looking as though you are on top of everything in life. This comes from the place of needing acceptance and love. 'Will people think less of me if I appear as anything less?'

Like myself, you obviously recognize the need for some balance in your life, evident by the fact you are still reading my book, and good for you by the way.

Understanding our why is the doorway to finding our way to a balanced life.

In this section of my book, we are going to look at other real-life situations from five individuals who have also achieved a black belt in control. However, after gaining a revelation from God, they found Him to be the 'God of more than enough', the 'God of the impossible', 'Jesus our deliverer', and they have put God back in His rightful position, as the true burden carrier.

As you read these stories, many of you will begin to see the pattern of how the enemy has used what we intended to be good, helpful and loving, to be in fact, a way of burning ourselves out. This can leave a trail of disunity, disappointment, anger, judgement, guilt and despair. This is the enemy's goal.

As I have mentioned already, these stories are true. Real life testimonies from brave souls who were willing to put their hand up and share their experiences with you in order for you to know that you are not a lone ranger in this quest of needing to hand over the reins of control to the true 'Way Maker'. These amazing people who have told me their story which I have written in this section of my book, I call 'brave' because it took a lot of guts for them to dig into their pasts, recall events and situations, bringing it all back up to the surface and face it once again. However, each one of them have said to me that they were willing to do this for you. My hope is that I have given their stories justice as I wrote them in the following chapters. Friends, take a breath and rest in the knowledge that you are not alone in this journey. There are many of us out there wrestling with this same issue.

The good news is, there is a pathway to freedom. There is a better way. Each of these stories have proven that. We too can have a positive outcome as we choose to face our so-called demons and allow God to stand in the gap and lead the way out.

I asked each of these five people four questions after which I have drawn key take away points for you to consider. Be inspired.

- What was the situation you felt you needed to control?
- What do you feel was the root cause of the need to be in control?
- How did you work with God, wrestle with God, to get a breakthrough in this area?
- Understanding that Jesus is your burden carrier, what was your process of handing over control of the issue or situations you have carried?

*Note: People's names changed for their privacy.*

# 9
## OUT OF THE ASHES – Elizabeth's Story

**What was the situation you felt you needed to control?**

All my life I believed I must be in control of everything at all times, lest my world fall apart. I grew up in the 1960's and in those days, particularly in my home environment, it was frowned upon to conceive a child at a very young age. Three of my four grandparents were also very controlling and had very rigid beliefs on how we should all live our lives. One of those beliefs was that children should be seen and not heard. As I reflect on my growing up years, I recognise that even as a young girl my external environment was very controlled. I was taught to fear everyone in authority. Parents, relatives, police, teachers, doctors, anyone who seemingly had a right to direct my life.

My sisters and I learned to obey our parent's instructions to the letter of the law. We knew what was expected of us. We were told repeatedly that we were to be 'good girls', and it was reinforced in no uncertain terms, that unless we were 'good girls', translated; 'always perfect in everything we did', there would be consequences. Those consequences instilled fear into us children. Fear for me led to feelings of anxiety and stress. Knowing what the penalties were, I would keep my antennae up, making sure I was always doing the right thing. At all costs, I had to make sure I portrayed the 'good girl' image for my parents, and the world to see, as was expected of me.

With such a tight control over my life, I knew that I needed to take control of every action and every decision I made, so as to please my family. I thought, 'If I take control of everything I do, I will be safe'. Everything had to be perfect and everything had to look perfect. Even our clothes and shoes had to be fastidiously cared for. Every time I made my bed, I would be careful to not have a single crease in my bedsheets or quilt cover. One time after meticulously tucking in my sheets, pulling up the quilt cover to just the right position, setting my pillows neatly at the top of my bed and straightening every corner of the sheets, one of my sisters came running into my room and intentionally pulled off all my bedding. I reacted dreadfully. I was so angry. I couldn't believe she would do that. I look back now and think how ridiculous my response was, but at the time, it was devastating because now everything was not 'just right', and what if my parents saw the mess before I had a chance to remake my bed.

Every school day my siblings and I had to bring home the wax paper my mother wrapped our lunch in otherwise we were severely reprimanded. Every detail of our home environment was very controlled and very regimented. The only thing I could control, was my determination to hide my feelings and responses, but it was exhausting!

Being the eldest daughter, the expectation on me was even greater. I would be told over and over again, 'You will be loyal. You will be reliable. You will be a leader. You will be responsible, accountable, dependable, and you will be strong'.

My father was in the military so the order he practiced in his work place also came into our home. Subsequently, control not only came from my mother, but also from my father. My parents controlled pretty much everything in my life during my growing up years and even after I got married.

In 1967 dad left to serve in the Vietnam war. I remember the day he left so vividly. It was in the early hours of the morning and while it was still dark, he came to me and said, 'It's your job to look after the girls'. I was six years old. I felt the weight of that directive immediately, and from that day on, I literally took on the responsibility of taking care of my sisters' every need. I not only did this for the twelve months my father was in Vietnam, but for decades after.

My father put this burden of responsibility not only on me, but my mother also. Our father was very abusive, and our mother was trying to survive in our hostile environment, so she leaned heavily on us her children for support, to the point I felt I was parenting her instead of her parenting me.

When I got married, I felt the control of my parents followed me. Whether it was realistic or not, I felt under constant pressure to make sure everything I did met the approval of my parents. I did not want to disappoint them. I wanted to continue to be that 'good girl' they told me over and over again I must be even though I was now out of my parent's home and living with my husband.

I rarely felt relaxed around my father. In fact, I believed he was in my head. I would hear him say, 'I know what you're thinking', and he was usually right. Those thoughts were a constant torment to me.

The layer upon layer of burden that my parents put on me, expected of me and insisted I be responsible for, all contributed to the belief that I needed to be in control of my life in every situation.

Married life presented brand new scenarios for me. I grew up with controlling parents and grandparents and the outworking of that in my life equated to me controlling how I felt at all times including not allowing my parents into that space. My husband however, although also coming from a controlling home, managed his life in a completely different way. He would always just 'toe the line', because for him, it was the least form of resistance and he wanted to make sure he had the love and acceptance of his parents. He chose to go with the flow on any and every decision his family made for him.

The controlling patterns of our families formed the foundation of how our marriage would work. For me who had suppressed control but desperately wanted it, and for my husband who had submitted to control because, 'Hey, why fight it', led to who took hold of the reins of our family. You guessed it - me. He preferred I lead in the relationship and it was second nature for me to lead and control as I learnt from the best, my parents.

This control behavior of mine became entrenched in every area of our marriage including bringing up our children. As our children grew up, it was me they would come to and depended on for pretty much everything. The message I continued to send out was, 'I am the one in control'.

I believed that while I was in control, I would be safe, and just maybe this meant my children would also feel safe. It was up to me to be their protector at all times.

I controlled who the kids hung out with, what they did, and where they went. I felt responsible for their behaviours, and although I may not have verbalised it or even consciously thought it, their behaviour was a reflection of me and my parenting, therefore I needed to be in full charge of everything they did.

My thought pattern was, 'If things went wrong with the kids then I must be to blame'. I now know that this came from continually being told by my parents when anything went wrong in our home, 'It is your fault'.

I realised however, that no matter how much I tried to protect my environment through control, I could not stop my children from making their own decisions. When my daughter chose to marry a man who we could see was a pure narcissist, I could not convince her to see that marrying this man would give her a life of grief. I wanted to stop her from making what I believed would be the worst decision of her life. This in itself was a good warning, however my daughter was of an age where she could make her own decisions, and she was determined to stick to the decision she had made. I found myself in a situation I could not control.

I love God. I know God. I know His power and His ability but it was so intrenched in me to think that I was the one who made the world go around in my family, that when I prayed to God for help, I would find it hard to give Him the reins of the situation. I would cry out to Him and His answer would always be the same, 'Trust Me with her'. I was at war with my feelings and what God was telling me to do.

**What do you feel was the root cause of the need to be in control?**

The root cause of me feeling I had to be in control at all times can definitely be attributed to the emotional fear placed on me as a child. Fear laced through every aspect of my life. From my parent's control, to a close relative's own personal issues with fear being outworked by hurling abuse towards me, leaving me feeling paralysed and with a sense of worthlessness. I was nothing, a nobody. The barrage of verbal abuse would reduce me to an emotional mess. I was my relative's scape goat. That fear was then expressed from within me through unhealthy behaviours and thoughts towards myself and others. The more I could not control situations, the more I felt the need to try and be in control.

The words, 'It's your fault', rang loud and clear when things went wrong in our home. I was to blame for failures and was held accountable by my father. Unreasonable expectations on a child who then grew up to be a woman racked with fear. I carried guilt, shame, feelings of worthlessness, low self-esteem and lacked self-confidence. I did not know my true identity so I learnt to always wear a mask projecting that all was well, however, behind closed doors it was anything but.

To be in control gave me a sense of safety. When I could control my internal and external workings, I felt I could survive. If I was in control then someone else wasn't in control of me. For me, that equated to freedom. Even as I write this, I see how distorted my thinking was.

**How did you work with God, wrestle with God, to get a breakthrough in this area?**

It wasn't until I was in my mid-thirties that I began to get a revelation.

Long after leaving home and getting married, I still felt the weight of responsibility for my siblings even though they too were getting married and starting to have families of their own. I began to take note of how my sisters were doing life as a nuclear family and caring for their own children which made me realise, I don't have to be their protector any more, they are doing just fine without me. I could just be their sister and be on an equal footing. I gave myself permission to do just that, be their sister.

A greater revelation came through the prayer and counsel I received from trusted people who prayed for burdens in my life to be lifted. The responsibility of being the older, protective sister had gone on for way too long and God opened my eyes to see that even my father could not punish me any longer if my sisters got themselves into trouble.

I read the Word of God, listened to sermons, came along side others who wrestled with their own issues and who needed a listening ear. I prayed and I listened and occasionally wrote down what I knew God wanted me to know for myself.

Regarding my daughter's situation, on a couple of occasions when desperately pleading with God to do something, and then adding, 'What can I do for her', He would say, 'Take your hands off her, she is mine'. My mother's heart would say, 'What? I trust no one except myself'. However, the reality was, I knew I had no answers in myself, so I had to trust Him. I had to hand over that control to God. I knew I had to obey God's directive. It's not to say I didn't worry or feel responsible at times. I was still tempted to spare her pain, rescue her, fix everything so she was happy within herself, but I learnt that I could not do what only God can do. My daughter was God's first and foremost and He loved her, knew her more intimately that even I do, and He would meet her where she was at in a way that I could never possibly do.

As I began to put my trust in God more, my prayers began to change. They moved from, 'God help, but now what can I do', to 'God, whom I choose to trust'. That was a big step for me. To acknowledge God as my heavenly Father who can do anything He chooses to. My Heavenly Father who loves me and accepts me just the way I am, a work in progress. He never judges me, He never asks unreasonable things of me, and is always available for me. He has all the answers to my requests and loves me unconditionally.

I had to unlearn what was so familiar to me, being the one in control, and choose to accept what Jesus did for me and receive ministry from the Holy Spirit and be obedient to His leading. My brain went through a process of rewiring and my emotions had to be challenged and healed. Although it was exhausting, because it caused me to feel very vulnerable and not in control, it needed to happen for me to become whole.

**Understanding that Jesus is your burden carrier, what was your process of handing over control of the issue or situations you have carried?**

This story isn't primarily about my relationship with my parents and the effect of their parenting. It's not even about my parenting. It's solely about my relationship with my spiritual Father. Who I am in Him. What He has done for me. What He gave up for me. Who He believes I am in His eyes. How much He loves me no matter what. I am the one who needed to change.

The control issue was debilitating me, it consumed my feelings and emotions, and depleted me. I would carry the weight of disappointment, shame and frustration which would then turn to anger. It would build up over time until eventually exploding out of me, reducing me to feeling empty and full of despair. I then had to find a way to recover. I would tell myself that God has the big picture in His sight, which I cannot see. I would remind myself that I had a choice; I could choose to torment myself with working hard to stay in control or relinquish that control to a higher authority. It was a constant cycle. I knew the latter was what led to true freedom and once I got a taste of that and practiced trusting in a faithful God, the easier it became. Jesus is my rescuer and Saviour, not me.

I needed to make the choice of allowing Jesus to be in control of my life, my circumstances and the decisions I made. I had to align with His will. I needed to be obedient and submit to God and His will for my life, leaving my family in His hands, knowing He had only the best intentions for them as well. Was that easy? Not at all. It was, and continues to be, a daily decision of my will, because to submit and obey had always equated to being under a person's control.

The good news is, whenever I have submitted myself completely to God, allowing myself to become vulnerable before Him, although painful at times, I have experienced the greatest change in my life. Each time I choose to accept the transforming power and love of my heavenly Father, a deeper bond of trust with Him is formed.

The recurring message I would receive from my Heavenly Father in the dark times was simply, yet profound, 'Trust Me'. I had to remind myself that I am my daughter's guardian, however, she is God's child. He has full control, not me. The fear that drove and fed the control I exercised in life was not driven by God. He tells me to not have a spirit of fear, but of power, love and a sound mind. I had been so worried, so distraught for years and years about not having control of her situation, but what was that achieving? All it did was leave me feeling hopeless in the situation, feeling powerless which caused me to feel frustrated and angry. These feelings did not help me feel close to God but instead the opposite. I knew all along I needed God and I knew He was patiently waiting for me to hand over the reins of control in my life to Him. I had to surrender!

It is still a work in progress; however, I can honestly say that I hand over to God the thoughts and feelings I have that burden me more easily these days. I am also pleased to say that rigid rules and control are a lot more relaxed than ever before. It has taken considerable time and practice to hand things over and often it's a daily surrender. I have to submit to Him what is His.

We all have our time of day that we are most sensitive to hearing from God. For me, it is at night, or should I say, the middle of the night. The time of day I best commune with God. I find myself chatting away to Him, just as I would to a friend, and at the same time, reciting and meditating on His Word. Philippians 4:6-7: 'Do not be anxious about anything, but in every situation, by prayer and petition, with thanksgiving, present your requests to God. And the peace of God, which transcends all understanding, will guard your hearts and your minds in Christ Jesus'. This scripture is one of my 'go to' verses during times of temptation of wanting to pick up the burden backpack. Each time I read this promise, it reminds me who my burden carrier is, and with that, I lay my head back on the pillow with confidence and return to sleep.

Everything we go through, God can use to help others. Opportunities present themselves for me these days where I am able to share my experiences with people who are currently walking the path I have. I can say to them with all honesty, 'I understand'. Having walked the road of, 'I have to control', to now submitting myself to a journey of trust, many doors are now open for me and I am finding many people are receptive because they know I 'get it'. They know that I understand the cycle of living in fear of letting go of control. When people hear my story, they are willing to receive the encouragement and wisdom from God who wants the best for them and those in their world also.

I have witnessed people close to me have break downs due to trying to be in absolute control with perfectionist tendencies. It has taken a destructive toll on them mentally and physically. I choose not to go down that path.

To control everything and everyone is exhausting and paralyzing. It is a fruitless exercise. It imprisons and distorts perspective and is isolating. In the past when not in control, I felt anxious and vulnerable which escalated to feelings of anger and frustration. That is not who I wanted to be. That is not how I wanted to be defined.

I am not my childrens' saviour, Jesus is. He is my childrens' refuge and their healer. By the whisper of the Holy Spirit, He is their counsellor, their comforter and wise leader. Jehovah Jireh is their provider. Jesus can be their everything, and He does not do it through control but by ever so gently, patiently and lovingly presenting Himself to each of them. I know that they will hear Him when they commune with Him.

I am free in Christ, my burden carrier. Many, many experiences in life reiterated that I cannot fix other people or their circumstances. I learned what my true purpose and role in life was concerning others and it is to pray for people, be available, come alongside them and listen to their heart. I don't have to be their enabler. I have to be Jesus to them. That is the most powerful, healthy, loving role to assume. Attend to others. Serve others but not control others or their situation.

KEY TAKE AWAYS

- Give yourself a permission note. 'I gave myself permission to be just their sister'. As you read this statement, did you find that it resonated with you? You need to give yourself permission to just be someone's sister or brother, someone's wife or husband, someone's daughter or son. Give yourself a permanent exemption from the titles, 'Burden Carrier or World Worrier'. The super hero who comes to save the day. We already have one of those and His name is Jesus.

> Whether the Holy Spirit comes with a soft whisper or a loud shout, His motivation is to get you to understand that when He speaks, He speaks truth, and the promises He makes with you, He will fulfill.

- It takes practice. Recognise that the journey to wholeness and trust is realising we can only arrive there by practicing habitual change. Exchanging anxiety for trust. Exchanging fear for faith. Exchanging control as we know it for God's control. The good news is, God is not controlling. He comes by offering His hand in a loving caring way and through soft whispers He says, 'I've got this'. I will say though, sometimes He needs to say it loud and if you are anything like me, loud is sometimes necessary. Whether the Holy Spirit comes with a soft whisper or a loud shout, His motivation is to get you to understand that when He speaks, He speaks truth, and the promises He makes with you, He will fulfil. I challenge you to start practicing prayer over anxiety. Let prayer be your default, not fear; knowing God hears and responds.

Philippians 4:6-7 says: *'Do not be anxious about anything, but in every situation, by prayer and petition, with thanksgiving, present your requests to God. And the peace of God, which transcends all understanding, will guard your hearts and your minds in Christ Jesus'.*

Note: According to data released by Amazon on the most highlighted passage in Kindle ebooks, the most popular passage from the Bible is this passage from Philippians. Most biblical scholars agree that the apostle Paul composed Philippians while he was in prison so the fact that Paul was able to reject anxiety even during his own imprisonment makes the passage all the more encouraging. Although it might seem novel to see biblical writers addressing modern worries, the lesson from this passage is timeless and can affect anyone. The life of faith is filled with constant challenge to risk more to become our true selves.

# 10
## HE IS MORE THAN ENOUGH – Daniel's Story

**What was the situation you felt you needed to control?**

My father was a toy salesman and he would often take us down to the Toy Factory on weekends to play with the toys. He would open up the display room and say, 'Go on boys, go play with as many toys as you want'. We had lots of fun and it was a great time in our lives. My father and mother loved us and cared for us immensely. They were the best parents a child could ask for. I always looked up to my dad for advice and I believed he would always be there whenever I needed him. I was sure those days would last forever. However, life as we knew it, was about to change.

The day began as any other day, with dad coming in to my bedroom and waking me up for school. He would give me a kiss on the forehead and tell me to have a great day. Yes, it was just like every other day. I went off to school and overall, the day was uneventful. When the school bell rang, sounding the end of the day, I raced down to the gate to meet my mother as I always did, but today, she wasn't there. I waited and waited, looking out for her but she didn't come. Not too long after, one of the teachers came running down to me to let me know that my mother wouldn't be picking me up today, but a neighbour would be coming to get me instead.

On the way home in the car, my heart began to drop because I just knew that something was wrong. Although my neighbour didn't say anything to me on the way home in the car, everything inside of me was saying, there is something not right about this day. I couldn't explain it, but I just knew I was going to be met with bad news. As we entered our small street and my house came into view, the picture explained itself. There were cars everywhere, even all over our lawn. I walked into the house and was greeted by my mother who took me and my siblings aside, sat us down, and told us that our father had had a heart attack and passed away.

So many emotions began to well up inside of me. Hurt, pain, and overwhelming anger. I was angry at God, angry at my mother, angry at my brothers and angry at the world. These feelings overwhelmed me to the point it became unbearable. It was then and there I made the decision to forget who my father was and push any feelings I had for him deep down inside of me. I vowed I would never let those feelings take control my life again. I thought to myself, I cannot control what has happened to my father so I am going to control how I feel about losing him, and over time I succeeded. I got to the point I could no longer remember who my father was.

At the age of twelve, just two years after my father passed away, my life began to spiral out of control. I began to smoke cigarettes with my mates and by the time I was thirteen or fourteen, I was dabbling in marijuana and alcohol, and often binge drinking on the weekends. Although my life was spinning out of control, I believed I was completely in control. I made sure my family didn't know what I was up to or how I was feeling. I became quite good at hiding both my lifestyle and my emotions.

The truth was, life for me only continued to spiral out of control and eventually I began using all kinds of illicit drugs. I decided that school was not for me and I informed my mother that I was leaving to which she responded, 'It's either school or full-time work'. I chose full-time work.

**What do you feel was the root cause of the need to be in control?**

I know the root cause of needing to be in control of my feelings came from the sense of abandonment. Not only did my father leave me at a young age, although no fault of his own, but at around this same time, one of my brothers left home and my mother went out to work seven days a week. I felt I had been deserted by everyone close to me. My mother was, and still is, a wonderful mother, and she would never have known my inner turmoil. However, no one spoke of the emotions that each one was going through. Everyone handled their grief in their own way and I was left to deal with mine, alone, and the only way I knew how, through drugs, allowing them to dull any memories I had of what I had lost.

**How did you work with God, wrestle with God, to get a breakthrough in this area?**

It began with a letter I received from one of my brothers. He began by saying, 'Hey mate, there is something in your life that you need to change. You can't keep going down this pathway. You can't keep living this lifestyle. You need to pull your head out of the sand and realise that you are not only hurting yourself, but you are hurting our mother and you are hurting us'.

I loved my mother and would never want to hurt her. However, because I was so self-absorbed in how I wanted to run my life, I didn't stop to think about what it was doing to her and the rest of my family. I didn't realise that the control I thought was protecting me, was actually hurting the people closest to me. These were the people who were always there for me, who always provided for me, who always helped me out. They were the first people who, when I was in trouble, would come and pick me back up again. I began to see that I not only pushed down memories of my father, but I had also pushed away emotionally, the very people who cared for me the most. I never really took into consideration that they too were hurting, just as much as I was. For the first time in a long time, uncontrollable emotions came flooding back in. I couldn't stop the flow of tears that overwhelmed me. I was broken.

It was around this time, a really cute girl turned up at my workplace looking for a part-time job. I was fortunate enough to be the one to greet her at the gate on her first day at work, and from that very day, I was smitten. It wasn't long before we began to interact and I thought, 'I am going to ask this girl out on a date'. It was a little bit awkward at first, but I finally got up the courage to ask her out. We had become friends so I thought it would be a done deal. When she answered back, 'NO', I was surprised, but I was not going to let her 'no' dissuade me, so I asked her out again, and again, and again. Her answer remained the same. 'No'. I decided I was just going to keep asking her out until her no turned into a yes, even if she said no one hundred times more. I couldn't believe it when eventually her no did turn into a YES. Little did I know at the time, that her yes was just to get me off her back and she had intended on backing out just before we were to go out.

Hours before we were to meet, she rang me to let me know that she just couldn't do it. Immediately my heart sank but she then went on to say, 'But hey, we have a big games night on at our youth group tonight if you would like to come'. My first response to that was, 'What's youth group?' She went on to explain it was where a heap of teenagers and young people got together. I think in her mind she thought I would say no, but straight away I said, 'Yes, I will be there'.

I arrived drunk and under the influence of drugs, but at the end of the evening as I walked out to the car park, about four or five guys came out to see me. They asked me my name and showed genuine interest and care towards me.

I began to go to church, but it was really just to chase after this girl. However, although I didn't know it at the time, God was chasing after me.

The turning point for me in handing over control was at an Easter Service. The pastor spoke about the love of God and the Father heart of God. It was in that moment, hearing those words, I realised that I was accepted by Him no matter what I had done, no matter where I had been. He knew my innermost being. He knew every emotion that was locked deep inside of me. At the end of the service, the pastor asked if there was anyone who wanted to receive Jesus into their life. I immediately put up my hand, went to the front of the church, and received Jesus into my life.

Although I gave my heart to Jesus at that time, every time after that when an opportunity was given for people to accept Jesus as Lord and Saviour of our lives, I would put my hand up. Every time, I would go out to the front for prayer, and give my heart to Jesus. I would do this over and over again. Eventually my youth pastor came to me and said, 'Hey, you know what, it is great that you have made a decision to turn your life around, but you keep putting your hand up, you keep coming to the front and you keep making this decision to follow Jesus, every single time. Can you tell me why you do that?'

I said, 'I can't understand how a loving God can forgive me for all the things I have done, all the pain I have caused, all the people I have ripped off, everything I have done wrong; in just one decision'.

My pastor took me aside, grabbed a whiteboard and marker and said, 'Tell me everyone you have hurt. Everyone you have ripped off. All your sins. Name all the people you have caused pain to. Write it all down. Everything you can think of that you have done wrong. Every area you have tried to control which has backfired'. As I spoke it all out, the pastor wrote everything on the whiteboard. It was all there in front of me. Then he said to me, 'This is what happens when you give your life to Jesus'. He went and got the whiteboard eraser and he wiped that whole board clean of everything I had done. He told me, 'This is what happens when you give your life to Jesus. He forgives you. He heals you. He takes your pain and sin, and He gives you a new heart and a new start'.

> *Psalm 51:7 (NLT) says: 'Purify me from my sins, and I will be clean; wash me, and I will be whiter than snow'.*

Hearing these words were both a relief and a release from the bondage I was holding myself to because I always believed I needed to earn acceptance rather than it be a free gift.

**Understanding that Jesus is your burden carrier, what was your process of handing over control of the issue or situations you have carried?**

The process is a daily walk. I had become so good at hiding my emotions for such a long time that even today, in my forties, I can get caught in the trap of pushing my feelings deep down inside of me whenever a situation arises that I find hard to bear.

The key is awareness. I have learnt to give myself a heart check. I have to have a chat to myself. I tell myself, 'You know what, you cannot control these emotions you have about this situation on your own, but with Jesus you can'. I ask Him to come and deal with those inner feelings, those inner thoughts, the situation, and help me work through them in a healthy way.

We can believe that no one else has walked this road, had these feelings, gone through what we have gone through or truly understands, so we hide our emotions and our thoughts. We tend to believe that if we share what we are going through with anyone, then maybe they will think we are weak or not capable of what God has called us to. However, the truth is, multitudes have walked these roads and it is those people who can help us through our own journey. It is those people who have come through what we have been through. We all have our struggles, but Jesus shines a light on them so we can start to walk in wholeness. Psalm 119:105 says: 'Your word is a lamp for my feet, a light on my path'.

Getting a word from God, leaning on Jesus, having people in your life who will stand with you and guide you is key.

## KEY TAKE AWAYS

- Face our emotional turmoil. One of the hardest things we can do in life is to allow those excruciating emotions to surface. We don't want to look at them because they are too raw and too painful. It is easier to let them fester in our heart than rip the band-aid off in order to heal. We just don't want to go there. It takes a brave soul to say, 'This is going to really hurt, but to become whole, I need to face these emotions and the turmoil I struggle with and allow Jesus to work with me to become whole. Jesus is my burden carrier. Jesus' portfolio is 'Burden Carrier'.
- Awareness. Once we become aware of our habits that are damaging to ourselves and others, we have to take responsibility to respond differently. We need to begin the steps to a new healthy habit. To help create this new pathway, regularly ask yourself these questions to stay on track; 'Am I taking a burden on that belongs to Jesus? Am I trying to wear a cloak that only Jesus can wear?'
- Don't be an island. We need people in our lives who can walk with us. Even talk the tough talk to us. I have them. I am grateful for those people. Do I like it when they give it to me straight? No, but I love them for it because I know they have my best interests at heart. Our job is to stay humble and teachable before God in the process of growing and we complete our growth when we meet Jesus face to face.
- You are not alone. The enemy wants to tell us we are the only ones who have this problem, or deal with this or that issue. The truth is, we all have struggles of one kind or another. Do something about it now before the enemy tells you it's too late.

# 11
## CAPTAIN UNDERPANTS – Claire's Story

**What was the situation you felt you needed to control?**

I'm a Supergirl 'undies on the outside, cape on' kind of girl. I always have been. I try not to be, but the trouble with me being a 'living sacrifice for God' in my own strength is that I keep getting up from the altar and walking away. I was convinced that if my hand was not on the wheel, things would not get done, wouldn't be carried out correctly, or injustice may occur. It's not a badge I wear with pride, but it is a theme that has permeated throughout my life for as long as I can remember.

I see myself as a square peg in a round hole. I have always needed to work hard to fit in. I am also one who will deny my own feelings in order to please others. I am one of those people who feels driven to take responsibility for situations which ultimately manifests itself in me becoming a control freak. I'm very happy to play second fiddle in a group, however I find it frustrating when there is no clear direction in an organisation or leadership team, or when I am part of a particular group where no one can make decisions. This is me.

What situation did I feel I needed to control, you ask? There was not one, but many situations which both triggered and contributed to the need of suiting up in cape and undies. You will need a coffee for my story!

I had a peaceful childhood, however at a very young age, my parents, who owned a motel expected that I, the firstborn, would help run the office, clean the units and organise bookings. Then at the age of thirteen, my siblings and I were sent off to boarding school and my responsibility for their happiness was assumed. How I personally felt about this new normal was not considered, and I was told in no uncertain terms not to complain because I was lucky to be going to boarding school and it was my duty to be in charge of my siblings. I felt anything but lucky. I was miserable, lonely and often cried myself to sleep.

My parents moved house several times during my boarding school years and then half way through my final and most important year, we moved countries. I was just expected to cope simply because I was bright and academic. Nobody considered how hard it was for me when I failed all my exams by two or three marks, which meant I then had to repeat that final year of school. After I finished my senior year at high school, I found myself fighting the education department for permission to enter university. I had to prove that I had the academic ability to study. Not only this, but I was told that if I failed even one subject over the next three years, then I would fail university. They even told me that my final year at high school would count for nothing. That four years of work would be lost.

This particular battle I needed to fight on my own because the alternative was to allow my father to argue the case on my behalf which would not have ended well for me. The phone calls to the education department would have been abusive and unproductive. When I turned to my mother for support, I was only met with hurt and disappointment. 'Just accept your fate', she would tell me. I internally needed to manage both my parent's responses while at the same time wrestle with the education department to get the outcome I needed from them in order for me to attend university. Those university years saw me fight and work long and hard, and thankfully I won. I am proud of myself for not giving up my dream because I was able to achieve not one, but eventually three degrees including a degree in social work. Imagine if I had just accepted what had been spoken over my life, 'Accept your fate'.

While studying at university, I met and married one of the finest human beings on the planet. A man with a kind heart and a generous spirit but who also came with a huge dose of what I later learnt was Asperger's Syndrome. His IQ was off the chart which was impressive, but it was his sense of loyalty and humour that attracted me to him. His emotional interactions with me however, were a different story, often leaving me feeling like I had been punched in the face. This was not because he was abusive in any way, but simply because his emotional response as an Asperger's type personality, meant there was no empathy or understanding when I needed that from him.

To understand what living with an Aspergers partner is like, you need to know that for a person who has this syndrome, they very often don't pick up emotional cues. In our marriage and in raising our children, I assumed responsibility for most of the emotional heavy lifting. It has been a sad, lonely and often ugly journey because very few people understand the dynamics of an Aspie/neurotypical relationship. My saving grace has always been knowing that Jesus does understand.

We tried for many years to have our first baby, which for me was very stressful. My Aspie husband on the other hand, was emotionally absent even during the times I would cry myself to sleep. After five long years, we conceived our first beautiful child, a daughter. I was overwhelmed with thankfulness to God for His gift to us. After the birth however, I developed a healthy dose of post-natal depression (PND), due to the birth being so traumatic which caused the natural mother-baby relationship between us to be quite tense. My burning sense of control took over and the need to be a perfect mother without fault dominated our mother-daughter relationship. I was not going to be one to have a noisy, sleepless, demanding, bottle-fed baby. My newborn was going to be perfect, just as I was to be the perfect mother. However, she was anything but. She was not quiet, not easy going and constantly pulled away from me when trying to breastfeed.

After two more babies and two more doses of PND with very little emotional support from my Aspie husband, my control mechanism gained traction. I was supposed to be the 'perfect mother' but here I was with PND. This led me to gaining two more members of my 'control company'. They were called guilt and shame. How could this be? A 'perfect mother' does not get anxiety and depression.

I had many internal struggles during my season of child-birth and child-raising, but despite these difficult times, God always came through. He put many amazing people in my life who were patient with me, prayed with me and walked with me through the dark days. Besides Jesus, they were my saving grace.

My parents eventually settled close to me, which I was pleased about, but my siblings moved away. Having them nearby seemed great at the time until my diabetic mum developed Alzheimer's. Dear old mum, or DOM as I used to call her, needed a lot of managing and here entered the conquering hero, me. I again put on my cape and my super-undies and off I went.

What followed were ten years of aged care, legal issues, managing the family trust funds, doctors, Dad's mood swings, mum's wandering, siblings who couldn't or wouldn't help out, two jobs, pastoring a church with no salary, working on my masters degree in social work, coping with blinding migraines, anxiety and then sinus infections. You could say, besides my super hero outfit, I also chose to wear many hats.

My doctor suggested I have my sinuses operated on. 'In and out overnight', the specialist said. What began as a simple sinus operation ended up being a perfect storm of staph infections and flu and to top it off, I was in burnout. My overnight stay turned into two weeks in hospital and due to the state of my mental health at the time, I found myself at home on the couch for two years. Literally.

It was during my two years of couch-time, a place where I was still and could do nothing, that God began to get hold of my heart. It was while I was in that dark place, I allowed God room to speak. He came and downloaded into my spirit the healing balm of understanding, revelation, and opportunity. The opportunity to learn about letting go, trusting in His faithfulness and me leaning in to whatever He wanted to say to me.

**What do you feel was the root cause of the need to be in control?**

The root of all our issues is usually believing the lie that we are better at ruling our lives than God is. I am great at pushing God off His throne so that I can have a go for a while, but as it turns out, He can rule the world perfectly well without my help!

Jesus said, 'I have come that you may have life, and have it to the full', John 10:10b. However, when we believe the lie of thinking we can do things without God's help, we allow ourselves to be controlled by the thief who comes to 'steal, kill and destroy', John 10:10a. My insecurities about false responsibility and control entered at pivotal points of trauma or vulnerability where I believed the lie that I needed to be in charge or responsible because nobody else was.

Abandonment was definitely another reason for me to feel the need to control. At the age of thirteen, our emotional development is supposed to be shaped by caring, responsible adults. However, they were not around because I was living at a boarding school. The emotional support I needed to navigate those formative years was absent and I wasn't receiving that from the school, which meant I was left fighting for survival, and carrying responsibility for my siblings. At boarding school, I was shaped very much by all the other teenagers living there who were also trying to figure out how to do life without proper guidance. We only had each other. Here we were, teenage girls who were trying to find our own identity but with no one leading us to find our way forward. Many of us felt that sense of abandonment at boarding school from our parents.

As an adult, my career path of counsellor and pastor created the perfect environment for this cloak of responsibility to be worn with pride. Over the years I have learned to put on my game face regardless of what was happening in my own life. I would take captive my own thoughts and feelings while bearing the emotional and physical burdens of others. Even during times of heartbreak, exhaustion, pain, anger or loneliness, I could craft my 'all is well' persona. I could hold my own tears back so I could hold the hands and tears of others. It has been like a drug allowing me to feel the exhilaration of being the saviour, the joy of being needed and the pride of being useful.

The sad truth about this scenario is that these control, saviour type issues, were not from God, but from the enemy, whose plan is to kill, steal and destroy what my Father had ordained for me. There is only one Saviour. And it's not me!

It was during my two years of 'Couch Time' where healing began. The Holy Spirit showed me the events which sowed the seeds of my need to control: The feeling of abandonment, being sent off to boarding school, taking on the fight alone for my place at university, battling to conceive my first child followed by a traumatic birth, my desperate loneliness during two bouts of post-natal depression, a simple operation turning into a nightmare of infections, caring for my mother during her many hospitalisations from broken bones to alzheimers, and her eventual death which for me felt like the ultimate abandonment.

You would think as a pastor and counsellor, I would have it all together, but don't be fooled. We are as vulnerable and broken as you are, just with a bit more frontline responsibility.

**How did you work with God, wrestle with God, to get a breakthrough in this area?**

In the natural, I felt abandoned, but God promises us that He will never leave us or forsake us. In Deuteronomy 31:8 it says, 'The LORD himself goes before you and will be with you. He will never leave you nor forsake you. Do not be afraid; do not be discouraged'. Hebrews 13:5 tells us, 'Keep your lives free from the love of money and be content with what you have, because God has said; Never will I leave you; never will I forsake you'. Joshua 1:5 reminds us, 'No one will be able to stand against you all the days of your life. As I was with Moses, so I will be with you; I will never leave you nor forsake you'. The promises of God can be relied on because He is true to His word.

It was my two years of couch time around 2015, during the most brutal but life-changing time, where the wrestle began. The infections had sapped all the energy from my very cells. Activities as simple as a shower would require five hours recovery and I could feel my energy draining out through my fingertips. I was not used to lying around. This wasn't who I was. I was used to putting in 200% even when running on empty and I was terrible at saying, 'no'. I was searching for answers and crying out to God to heal me, but there was no answer. Nothing! The silence was deafening. I couldn't pray. I couldn't read. I couldn't cry. All I could do was listen to worship music and read my Bible. I was losing weight, (not in a good way), my hair was falling out, I had terrible brain fog and I stopped sleeping. Three months in, DOM (mum) passed away. I raised myself off the couch to help her in hospital but the last time I did that, I paid a heavy price for it physically. The very last time I saw her was the day that the Lord told me to get up and go and see her. He even told me the time I needed to be there, 4pm. I used every ounce of my energy to get up and go, however, I missed her death by ten minutes. I had prayed that I could be with her to hold her hand as she passed away, but I missed it. Now I was grieving for her, for me, for my life and for my energy. I was angry. I felt lonelier than ever, I had no income, bills were piling up and my Aspie hubby wasn't happy. My father didn't understand. Nobody came to visit me for several months and I was crying out, 'Is this going to always be my life?' My GP said I was depressed and I would take seven to ten years to recover, a diagnosis I railed against, so I began searching for answers and I screamed at God, 'I WANT MY LIFE BACK!!!' His reply was sobering. *'Do you really?'*

That pulled me up. Right there and then, I began the life-changing conversation with my beautiful Lord. He said to me, *'Stop your moaning, I am giving you long service leave'*. Wow! He then, over the following few months, downloaded truth into my spirit – His truth. While He was pouring life blood into my life, He was, at the same time, unpicking the lies, like old thread. I'm a visual learner so that's how He teaches me.

He showed me a picture of a wooden cart full to overflowing with sacks. The wheels had broken and all the sacks spilled over the road. Each sack was a burden I was carrying, but now they were scattered. *'I'm not going to let you pick them up again'*, He said; *'But I do have a little wagon which you can put two or three sacks into at a time. Each time you pick up a sack, you must consult Me first'*. I learned how to come to Him for strategy through journaling and prayer and listening for the still small voice of the Holy Spirit. As I unpacked and offloaded the sacks, I felt freer.

He showed me a stream of crystal-clear water whose current was gentle and would carry me downstream. But the banks were marshy and muddy with rocks and reeds where my feet stumbled and I had to wade through the mud. The Lord asked me, *'Why do you keep wading through the marshes when I have given you the clear stream which is refreshing, cool and sweet?'* I had to learn to stay in the stream and away from the muddy banks because there I didn't have to strive, I could just drift with His current.

He asked me if I could identify myself in the story of Mary and Martha. Sadly, I could. I learned how to ask the Holy Spirit about the root of problems in my life, both physical and psychological. He showed me how to see those roots as shapes, pictures, and occasionally demonic forces. I came to realise that I was so busy 'doing', that I didn't know how to rest.

He showed me another vision of a belief I held, where my anxiety was linked to fear, and hence the need to control. In this vision I saw a baby being dangled by the ankles out of a second storey window. I looked and realised the baby was me and that the devil was dangling me way above the ground threatening to drop me. I was terrified of the freefall. My anxiety problems were rooted in my fear of freefalling. Then God invited me to look at that vision a second time to see the truth. I looked, and through my tears I saw that it was God holding me, rescuing me, not dangling me, and that His other mighty hand was right below my body. The truth was, there *was* no freefall! There would never be any freefall. He was above and below me, always there. I began the process of asking for forgiveness, to exchange the lie for the truth. It's the truth that will set us free.

He showed me my 'energy line' like a computer battery. If I crossed that line, it would result in me ending up back on the couch. God doesn't cause that, I do it to myself. He allows it if I choose not to rest and recharge. He reminded me that it is the small foxes which ruin the vineyard, as we read in Song of Songs 2:15. Just like those sacks. God requires us to only carry the sacks He hands us, not to load up on every little sack that may need to be picked up, but not by *me*!

I saw Jesus, cradling me like a small child, in His arms. And as I got better and stronger, I saw myself growing but always with Jesus.

**Understanding that Jesus is your burden carrier, what was your process of handing over control of the issue or situations you have carried?**

Jesus asked me if I was willing to surrender to Him. Surrender is a tough word for a control freak. The conversation went something like this, 'Could you give me a clue how that might look first? What might I be giving up? What will I be missing out on? What would you be asking of me?' Do you see what I'm doing here, dear reader? Yep, trying to control His offer. Clearly, I had learned very little. So, He showed me a doorway which was in the clouds and asked me whether I was willing to step through into His plan. I looked and there was nothing beyond the door, only clouds and what looked like freefall. Yikes! Yet, His promise to me was, 'You are my child and I will not let you fall. There is no freefall'.

If there is no freefall and I am His child, will I be safe if I step through the door when I can't see anything on the other side? How do I control this? The simple answer was, I could not. It was a scary position for me to find myself in. However, I knew if I really wanted to grow, I had to step through that door. I made the choice to trust God and walk through that doorway even though I didn't have all the answers. My emotions were racing and I felt completely out of control, but the moment I did step through, I couldn't believe what happened next. I suddenly felt a thousand times lighter and I was filled with incredible joy. The anxiety was lifted, and a real sense of relief flooded into my spirit. Who would have guessed!?

We never really understand the depths of the Father's love and compassion for us until we have come to the end of ourselves and have nowhere else to turn. This is what was revealed to me during my sacred couch time. It is only when we truly let go, that we learn that His hands are still underneath us, holding us up, bearing with us, just as a mother cradles her child. He offered me the choice. 'Do you want to let go and let Me hold you, or do you want to continue as you are?' I made the choice to let go.

It was so significant that I decided that I could trust Him with other things. My need for a new job, (my previous employers weren't keen on waiting two years for me to get off the couch). Achieving my Master's Degree in Social Work. Allowing His Spirit to wash over me to heal me of my firstborn birth trauma and the grief of abandonment. The greatest of all lessons I learnt though, was the lesson of how to rest and wait. This was the hardest, but I came to enjoy resting and to this day, I value rest. I prioritise it. I schedule it in as a gift to myself.

The day He asked me if I wanted my energy back I really had to think about it. Did I want my old life back? I wanted to join the world again, but I didn't want my old life back. I wanted deeper. I wanted more of Him and less of me. I wanted to trust Him without hesitation and lay down the need for control. So today, I find myself with about 95% of my energy which I try to use wisely. I'm back at work two - three days a week and loving life. I know what my core business on this planet is, and that is to minister to broken women, but I needed to let Jesus do that in me first.

I work daily to lay down my will in favour of His and to allow Jesus to carry my burdens and worries. I'm pleased to report I no longer suffer anxiety because I am quicker at handing over my worries, burdens and responsibilities to Jesus. I'm practicing saying 'no', with His help and I often plan my calendar with Jesus. It's always a choice, but I'm finding it easier every day. These days I keep the over-undies and the cape packed away in the cupboard and try not to bring them out for a special occasion. I'm constantly checking in when I recognize that I am beginning to struggle, taking time to look at the root of the struggle. I lay it before Him and ask Jesus to be in control again. I'm more chilled, moving slower and trying not to sweat the small stuff. I'm not perfect, but I am glorious in His eyes, and that's enough for me. I have a deeper sense of who I belong to and the incredible price Jesus paid for me. I am grateful. All glory to Him who reigns forever.

KEY TAKEAWAYS

- Who is going to define you? Don't let others' expectation of you determine the path God has for you. If Claire's mother's words, 'Just accept your fate', had been allowed to dominate who she was, giving her the title of 'I am a person who just accepts my fate' then her decision to press for a place at university may well have not happened.
- God can rule the world without your help. How often do we push God off the throne of our lives? We don't intentionally do that, but every time we think we know better or can't wait for God's timing, it is actually what we are doing. I love what Claire shared regarding our position. 'The root of all our issues is usually believing the lie that we are better at ruling our lives than God is. I am great at pushing God off His throne so that I can have a go for a while, but as it turns out, He can rule the world perfectly well without my help'.
- Do you really want your old life back? Or do you want to move forward and live life free of heavy burdens, free of carrying unnecessary sacks and being the saviour when clearly that is not your portfolio?
- There is no freefall. God does not tell us to step out and trust Him and then drop us to our death. His promise is sure. Psalm 121:3 says: 'He will not let your foot slip — He who watches over you will not slumber'.

# 12
## PEACEKEEPER – James' Story

**What was the situation you felt you needed to control?**

Having grown up in a large Irish Catholic family broken by alcoholism, I learnt at a young age how to read a room and then be whatever I needed to be to keep the peace. My father's alcoholism created a lot of fear in our household and I found myself overly sensitive to emotional discord, so I would do everything I could to smooth things out and keep everyone safe in the home.

**What do you feel was the root cause of the need to be in control?**

My fear of conflict and my inability to keep the peace at home when I was a child was the catalyst that sent me down the path of trying to minimise conflict in my life and the lives of others. I wanted everyone to be safe. I couldn't stop my dad from drinking, which to me, was the reason there was so much turmoil at home. I believed that the only option left for me was learn how to deflect his anger when he was drunk. Being the second oldest child of eight children, I felt responsible for my younger siblings and I didn't want to see any of them get hurt. Looking back on that time in my life, I can see how my desire to keep others safe steered me into an unhealthy path relationally that would soon start to unravel when Jesus reentered my life in my late teens and early twenties.

At the age of eighteen, I left home and joined the army. It was during my time there, that I reconnected with Jesus and things started to get interesting for me. I began attending an Assemblies of God church and soon became involved in the church's youth group. Eventually, I became part of the youth leadership.

As I progressed in leadership within the church, I found my talent for navigating social situations, and keeping everyone safe and happy, helped me to make friends and opened up opportunities to serve. After attending Bible College, I assisted two of my Bible College colleagues in planting a church. There I took up the position of youth pastor, working and building the church for several years. I was then given the opportunity to become an assistant pastor at a church in another state which led me to eventually pastoring my own church. I have now returned to the very state where my youth pastor days began. In each place I served, I would apply my 'keep everyone safe and happy' ability. So far it was working.

**How have you worked with God, wrestled with God to get a breakthrough in this area?**

In a perfect world, progressing in ministry would have been a wonderful process, after all, I was working with people who knew Jesus, and God was growing the expression of my gift and opening up doors of opportunity for me. In reality though, it was a far cry from the idyllic dream that I had fostered in my heart during Bible College. I started to come up against situations with people that I couldn't control; people who did and said things that hurt others. In the past when faced with difficult people outside of my family, I would quietly withdraw and move on with life, but time and time again I would find myself stuck in situations that I had to remain in, with people I didn't agree with.

What made it especially difficult, was when these people, who were in a position of leadership, lacked wisdom in how they went about treating others. My peace keeping ability in these situations was not working.

Other situations would come up where my peacemaking talent was not working either. I would come across a person who was acting in a way that was hurting themselves or others, but they would not take any advice I was giving them. I would be wanting to plan an activity or event but would come up against resistance, road blocks. On numerous occasions, these kinds of situations would come up and the end result would always be the same, I would hit a bottleneck and couldn't see a way forward in the relationship. Over and over again God brought me up against dead ends where my natural ability to smooth things over no longer worked and I was forced to make a choice between quitting the relationship or surrendering the situation to Him.

**Understanding that Jesus is your burden carrier, what was your process of handing over control of the issue or situations you have carried?**

It was at this stage in my life that I learnt a lesson that has stuck with me to this day - the art of surrendering relational bottlenecks to God. The strength I had depended on in the past, no longer seemed to work, but in the process, I found that when I surrendered the situation to God, He was able to do more than I could ask, think or even imagine.

It was here that I discovered that even though I couldn't change another person, God was always able to make a way in whatever relational situation I was faced with. I saw, over and over again, that even when I couldn't keep people safe, God was more than able to.

I still don't like conflict. Personally, I don't think you should be in leadership if you do. However, I'm not as concerned with managing it as I used to be. I realise I don't have to keep the peace in every situation, Jesus is the Prince of Peace, I'm just his bag carrier. It makes for a much less stressful life when you learn that He is more than capable of dealing with any relational situation you face in life or ministry. So far, He's never let me down. It's not a bad thing to want to see people flourish and thrive in life, but thinking that you can control every situation and protect people from conflict is a no-win game. I'm much quicker to ask God for his help than I used to be and I'm also able to leave people in His hands without worrying over the outcome. When you stop trying to control every outcome, you discover why He's called the Prince of Peace.

KEY TAKEAWAYS

- We can't continue changing our stripes in order to keep the peace. There is a big difference between peacekeeper and peacemaker. When we are peacekeepers, we adopt the management approach, putting the fire out at any cost. Peacemakers choose the solution approach even if it is tough. Galatians 1:10 says; 'Am I now trying to win the approval of human beings, or of God? Or am I trying to please people? If I were still trying to please people, I would not be a servant of Christ'. James, whose story we just read, learnt the lesson of moving from peacekeeper to peacemaker, and in the process, gained peace himself.
- It doesn't matter what walk of life we are in: ministry, business, school, homemaker or something else, we are always going to have people in our life. Learning the art of being a peacemaker will save you a lot of hard work.
- James mentioned that he was now only the bag carrier for Jesus. There is a difference between being a bag carrier and the burden carrier. For a start, the bag still belongs to Jesus, just as the burden belongs to Him. Jesus may hand over to you part of the problem to solve, but the good news is, it will come with Jesus' instructions to follow. He desires the outcome to be successful.

# 13
## LETTING GOD TAKE CARE OF THE CURVE BALLS – Leah's Story

**What was the situation you felt you needed to control?**

*Everything!*

My relationship with control is like so many others who have a strong default to take charge of, and control a situation that looks like it is threatening my personal world. You know it is not a good tendency to have, but you believe that for things to be right, it is up to you to take the reins. For me, I believed that as long as I held the reins of any given situation, it would be easier, less stressful and I would achieve the best outcome for myself and everyone else. With me in control, I could be sure things would be done how I wanted them done and within the timeframe I felt comfortable with.

I am one who sees potential risks before they happen which is a great aptitude to have. However, I would always find myself on guard in any situation, ready to pounce and curb any unwanted disasters. I found myself in a constant state of tension because I did not wish for any unwanted surprises.

Over the past ten years however, I have had a few unwanted surprises thrown my way. Real curve balls, which caught me off guard. My first marriage ending was one of those unexpected turn of events. Our marriage started out great. We had wonderful plans for our future including becoming foster parents, just as my parents had done when I was growing up. All that changed however, when I found out that my then husband was using illicit drugs. I was devastated. It changed everything. All our plans went out the window when it became obvious that my husband's love affair with drugs gave him more enjoyment than his love for me and commitment to our marriage. When confronting him with his habit, he made many promises of giving it up only to be followed by those promises quickly being broken. We tried counselling but to no avail and ultimately, our marriage ended in divorce.

During this turbulent marriage I desperately wanted to take control of what was happening, but no matter what I did, I realised this situation was completely out of my control. I felt out of control. You can imagine my stress.

One year after my divorce, I was blessed to meet and marry a wonderful man who had previously been an active Christian. Although he was away from the Lord when we began dating, I knew in my spirit that he had a genuine, caring and sincere heart. It wasn't too long after we married, I began to witness his incredible journey back to faith and he is now a fully committed man of God.

In marrying him I took on the role of stepmother to his two children and we have since had two more children of our own. Life was wonderful. I now had the life I always wanted. It was controllable and predictable, or so I thought.

It wasn't too long though before my family came under attack in ways I would never have predicted. First my brother was hit by a car and sustained a compound fracture. Then my mother developed a brain abscess and ended up in intensive care followed by three months in a rehabilitation unit learning how to breathe, talk and walk again. Immediately I found myself taking control of everything that needed to be done. After all, this was my role, or so I believed. I needed to do all the running around, be the messenger between family members, the one to reassure all involved that everything would work out, and stay on top of all the dramas throughout the course of these two crises for the sake of everyone else. *I* needed to…you get the picture.

During this time of seemingly having all the family situation ducks lined up in a row, the reality was, I felt totally out of control. I tried to hide my internal turmoil with an 'I'm fine' mask, but evidently those who knew me well weren't buying it. They knew I was anything but fine. One Sunday morning, while in the carpark about to head into church, our pastor stopped me and looked me straight in the eye and said, 'This is not yours to control.' I just looked at him and nodded politely. Again he repeated lovingly but firmly, 'This is not yours to control'. As he said it a second time, he gave me a big bear hug and immediately I burst into tears. Not nice little girly tears, but big loud ugly tears. I answered, 'If I'm not controlling this, who can? None of my family have ever stepped up before, I'm always the one they turn to for answers. If I don't have the answers, it means we are without direction'. I cried big time that day. I tried to go in to church but I was completely undone. The floodgates had opened and there was no closing them.

Another curve ball that came into my life was when I fell pregnant with our first child. While I was pregnant, I became very ill. I contracted pre-eclampsia which eventually developed into HELLP (Hemolysis, Elevated Liver Enzyme Levels, Low Platelet) syndrome. Without going into too many of the horrid details, it is a very dangerous and often misdiagnosed condition. I had to have an emergency caesarean to deliver my baby at thirty-three weeks, and the closest facility was a small outer suburbs hospital. Everything escalated from there. There were complications for my baby and for myself. There were many serious ups and downs for us both and needless to say, I again found myself in a place of being completely out of control. The crisis was a real test of my need to be in control in a completely out of control situation.

Our son was a real gift and a joy to my husband and I, but the first four years of our son's life was also a real struggle. Although he was a fun-loving kid, he also came with ongoing complications and a big dose of Autism.

I knew I could not fix this situation. Over a four-year journey, I swung between putting my trust in God and defaulting to, 'If I don't fix this, who will?' I knew that on my own, I was not winning. I eventually realised that while I continued to control this situation which only God could take care of, I was actually meddling in His divine work. I was hindering what He was wanting to do in my life and the life of my family. What a revelation that was. While I tried to be the burden lifter, I was hindering the work of the Father. I had to release my son and all we were walking through with him, to God, knowing He would lead us and guide us, as well as provide for us in every way.

**What do you feel was the root cause of the need to control?**

Needing structure and fear of not being prepared.

I was raised by loving, yet distant parents; both professionals in the medical industry, very intelligent and both high achievers. I have two biological siblings and one adopted sibling. My parents also took in many foster children throughout our growing up years. They took on the hard cases that no-one else would, often babies with extremely high needs. My siblings and I learnt to be grateful for the loving home we had and didn't complain when the others were given so much more attention.

When I turned eight years old, our family began to move around. Firstly, we went to a war-torn island near Papua New Guinea, then later, to a remote Aboriginal community in central Queensland. In these two places we saw firsthand the poor conditions of how people lived and it made us even more grateful for what our family had. Eventually we moved to Brisbane where we settled, but it was here that my siblings and I were often left home alone. My mother continued to travel for long periods of time for her work and I assumed the responsibility of taking care of my siblings even though I had an older sister. No one else seemed to be stepping up to the plate of taking charge, therefore I did. I told myself that if I didn't take control of things in the home, no one would. Even my father came to me asking me to solve issues regarding the running of the house. I believe it was at this point I took on the burden of being the saviour to the people in my life.

I recently saw a psychologist to explore my control issues. I was actually surprised to hear my parents referred to as absentee parents. It all made sense as we explored the topic and how my attempts at perfectionism and control was all to do with the lack of my parents love, affection and stability in the home.

To answer the question again, 'What do you feel was the root cause of the need to control?' I see now, it was all to do with desiring to gain the love and affection of my absentee parents. I also believe, that being in a home of absentee parents and with no one in my family taking responsibility for the running of the home, I assumed that responsibility. I took on the burden of bringing structure and organization to our household. A burden which should never have been mine to hold at such a young age.

**How have you worked with God, wrestled with God to get a breakthrough in this area?**

I had a great big tantrum with my Heavenly Father.

When the plans I had for a perfect life with my wonderful new husband and the children we would birth together in the future turned out not to be as perfect as I had imagined, you could say, I got a little angry.

I remember one time while I was in hospital with my tiny preppie son, his temperature soared through the roof and I cried out to God telling Him, 'You need to take this one for me God. I have no more energy. I can't face another round of scary news for my son'. I was sick of proving I was strong enough. I returned to my own hospital room and fell asleep from complete exhaustion. When I woke up I went back to the Neonatal Intensive Care Unit to see how my son was doing and to my surprise,

I was told that all his pathology tests were clear, his temperature had gone back to normal and there seemed to be nothing wrong with him. This was my wakeup call. I didn't have to prove anything. While I was resting, God was on the job.

Through the four-year journey working with doctors to get a final diagnosis of what our son's condition was, and through watching our son have test after test, operation after operation followed by more tests, took me to the edge. To put you in the picture, one major issue he had was craniosynostosis which is a fancy way of saying his skull fused together too early and he needed a skull reconstruction. Every time we got news from further testing to find out what was wrong with our son, it would always be negative. The doctors would call us in and I would brace myself for what was about to be said. I found it easy to lift the issue to God, however, letting go and trusting Him, was where I struggled every time.

**Understanding that Jesus is your burden carrier, what was your process of handing over control of the issue or situations you have carried?**

The day I received the doctor's letter confirming my son's diagnosis of Craniosynostosis, I also had my Bible app, 'Verse of the day' open. It was Joshua 1:9: 'Be strong and courageous, do not be afraid'. It comes from God calling Joshua to take Moses' place when he died. Preparing him for the battle to come.

Through all of this, my husband and I learnt to pray. We learnt the power of Romans 8:26 (MSG): 'Meanwhile, the moment we get tired in the waiting, God's Spirit is right alongside helping us along. If we don't know how or what to pray, it doesn't matter. He does our praying in and for us, making prayer out of our wordless sighs, our aching groans'.

I learnt not to hold things to myself, knowing I don't have all the answers and don't have to have all the answers. I know I don't even have to be articulate when talking to my Father God because without words, just groans and tears, He understands. I would be in the shower unable to form words to God but as I groaned and tears flowed, I knew that the

Holy Spirit was interceding on my family's behalf. He knew my heart. He knew my fear and He kept me strong throughout it all. I was no longer trying to be the hero, trying to save the day alone. We also had our whole church praying for us and with us.

I learnt to sing out a declaration of thanks to God. I would sing the song, 'In Jesus Name' by Darlene Zschech, a song I am so thankful for. When I didn't know what to pray, I would sing this song believing, that in Jesus name, everything would work out according to His perfect plan.

I sought His reassurance from trusted people. We had prophetic words, great Bible verses and an amazing church family who constantly reminded my family of God's promises.

As I have walked this journey, I have learnt that the only things I need to control are my responses to situations and to make the choice to put my faith in God to handle them. I control how I look up to Him, lift my situations up to Him and then let go, to allow Him to complete His perfect work.

Those times I have been able to let go completely, have been amazing. I have seen God take control of situations and manifest things I wouldn't have believed possible, or things eventuate with such little effort. It may have required some work and vigilance on my part, but now I never have to force a situation.

When I've let my guard slip or notice that I am starting to take control back, I do a reset. I hand back to God what is His to control. I'm constantly being referred back to Proverbs 3:5-6: 'Trust in the Lord with all your heart and lean not on your own understanding; in all your ways submit to him, and he will make your paths straight'.

## KEY TAKEAWAYS

- It is not yours to control. Those words Leah's pastor spoke that day in the carpark, may just be a lifesaver for you right now. 'It's not yours to control'. Let this be a relief valve for you. 'It's not yours to control'. You may be thinking just as Leah did, 'If I am not controlling this, who can?' You don't have to be everyone's answer and as I have said previously in this book, the world will not fall apart if you take your hands off the steering wheel. Psalm 56:3 tells us, 'When I am afraid, (because that is where the need to control comes from - fear), I will put my trust in you'. In other words, I may feel fear, I may feel out of control, but I choose to believe that You God, still hold the world in Your hands, and You still hold my situation in Your hands.

- Learn to rest in the storm. Jesus slept in a small boat while there was a storm. The disciples panicked in the storm. Why? The reason was because all that the disciples could see was the storm. Jesus rested because He knew the storm would not overtake them. Read Mark 4:35-41. Leah shared with us that while she rested, God was on the job. You can rest in the knowledge God is on the job for you.

> I may feel fear, I may feel out of control, but I choose to believe that You God, still hold the world in Your hands, and You still hold my situation in Your hands.

- Much more can be achieved when a situation we are dealing with is put into God's hands. The story of the young boy with five loaves of bread and two fish is a perfect example. While this food was in the boy's hands, he had just that, five loaves of bread and two small fish, enough food for himself. When he put those elements into the hands of Jesus, those loaves and fish fed five thousand people. Read John 6:1-14. While your situation is in your hands alone, it doesn't change. Put into the hands of Jesus, and He creates a miracle.

**THANK YOU TO THESE BRAVE SOULS FOR SHARING SO OPENLY AND HONESTLY FOR US ALL TO GLEAN FROM.**

# 14
## THE ROOT OF CONTROL

There are so many key take aways we can gain from the stories of these wonderful people. Don't you agree?

If you haven't realised it already from reading these incredible testimonies, the root cause of this type of control is FEAR. Fear tells you, 'You cannot let go'. It screams in your ear, 'Can you really trust God to rescue you, or the person or persons needing 'rescuing' from failing or falling? This situation is too insurmountable to be left at God's feet! What if God does not orchestrate things to turn out fair or just?'

The bottom line here is that you are believing a lie and questioning, 'Is God enough?'

If you have a relationship with God yourself, verbalizing those words out loud, 'God are you enough?' may cause you to be unexpectedly surprised, and even grieved at the idea of thinking that God is not big enough to meet your needs in any situation. You know God. You know the power and authority of God, but deep down inside, you are still wondering, 'Is God enough for my situation?'

The truth is, God is more than enough. He is not only enough, but can do vastly more than we expect. Ephesians 3:20 tells us, 'Now to him who is able to do immeasurably more than all we ask or imagine, according to his power that is at work within us'. I can imagine a lot, but more often than not, it is never enough. Our focus must move from what I can do, to what God, who can do the above and beyond, can do.

> The reason we can confidently shift our focus from us to God, is because His word is truth. Psalm 119:160 (NLT) says: 'The very essence of your words is truth; all your just regulations will stand forever'. Bottom line, once He declares it, it is done!

The reason we can confidently shift our focus from us to God, is because His word is truth. Psalm 119:160 (NLT) says: 'The very essence of your words is truth; all your just regulations will stand forever'. Bottom line, once He declares it, it is done!

# LESSONS I HAVE LEARNT IN MY JOURNEY OF LETTING GO OF CONTROL

## PEOPLE ARE MORE RESILIENT THAN WE REALISE.

By taking my hands off the person grappling with a situation which I have habitually jumped into, I have observed an amazing reality, they don't die on me! They may crash, burn, struggle, cry or feel hopeless, but in the midst of it all, just like the caterpillar battling its way out of a cocoon, they emerge stronger, more confident, with beauty and grace, and they begin to soar. Their struggle has birthed resilience, wisdom, knowledge and capabilities they didn't know were in them. They dig deep wells of their own. Guess what? I didn't do that. God did.

## MY FEAR, IS NOT NECESSARILY THEIR FEAR.

As a person who wants to rescue others from pain, mistakes and unnecessary challenges, I realise, the dramatic movie I am watching unfold in my mind may not necessarily be playing in the mind of the person with the dilemma. I have learnt I need to change from being 'The Saviour, I will do it, I will fix it, I will take it on for you', to, 'The Enquirer', asking questions to empower them. Questions like, 'How do you feel about this?' 'What do you want to do about this?' 'Can I assist?' Sometimes, I simply need to stay silent.

## THEY ARE GOD'S CHILD FIRST AND FOREMOST.

Oh surprise! Maybe you already know this, but isn't it ironic how we can know something to be true, and yet, believing and acting upon this truth is sometimes much harder to put into practice. Reminding ourselves of this reality is important, and this alone should stop us in our tracks, allowing ourselves a moment to re-evaluate the situation in light of God's love for the person, or people we are trying to fix, change, assist or control.

## I HAVE A CHOICE.

God has given us a free will, which means we can choose what path we want to walk. We can continue in the pattern of life we have allowed ourselves to be swallowed up in, or we can choose the better path, only doing what is required and helpful without controlling, which then creates room for God to move. Choosing not to jump in when the issue seems to be taking too long. Being willing to adjust your sails if things don't work out the way you planned it in your head. Remember, God's ways are higher than our ways, His thoughts are higher than our thoughts. Maybe, just maybe, He knows best. Listening to His whisper and obeying His voice in the situation, will free you from your emotional turmoil. It will give you peace to know there is one with a greater power, and His name is Jesus. He, who is the name above every other name, has got this!

# 15
COVID-19

Before moving on, I felt the need to add this particular section to my book because at the time of writing this, we are right in the middle of the COVID-19 pandemic. If there was ever a time to talk about our feeling of being out of control, it has to be the day COVID-19 came into our world. Not just landing on our own doorstep, but onto everyone's, worldwide. This planet as we have known it, changed almost overnight, and some things may never be the same again. How does that make you feel?

The devastation of COVID-19 in itself has been horrific. Countless lives lost. Weeping in the streets as family after family lost members to this terrible pandemic. Hospitals overflowing with patients and health workers overwhelmed by not only the number of cases they have dealt with, but the daily deaths that surrounded them. Jobs and businesses have been lost and families have been separated by borders and even countries. People stranded at airports, and in countries not their own. Schools closed and home schooling becoming the norm for parents and carers with school aged children, whether they were equipped or not. Our daily life, our security, the things that we held as a sure thing, suddenly gone, or at least changed.

I could go on, but my point is this, when we are in a situation where we have literally no control of circumstances, such as this COVID-19 pandemic, what is our response? Sure, this is an 'out of the ordinary' predicament, but what is our thought process in it all? Which direction do you take when something like this comes along? There is a quote by Elizabeth Edwards, who is an American attorney, a best-selling author and a health care activist, which I think sums up exactly how we should respond. It says, 'She stood in the storm, and when the wind did not blow her way, she adjusted her sails'.

How many of us have needed to adjust our sails throughout the COVID-19 season? How many chose to adjust their sails? When we learn to adjust our sails, we don't let such unexpected circumstances overwhelm us. Instead of cowering in fear, ask God this question, 'What should I do now?' rather than the why question, 'Why is this happening?' The 'why' may need to be investigated by those in authority, our governments and scientists. However, for you and I, adjusting our own sails gives us leverage to handle the changing winds.

What does 'adjusting our sails' look like? Many have said that COVID-19 has been a time of reset for us all. So, what has the COVID-19 season taught us? It can't be a season where we say, 'When this is over I can…' Of course, we want the season to pass, however, the better questions to ask are, 'OK God, what should I do now? What can I do differently because of what I have learnt in this season? What can I let go of? What insights have I gained into pinpointing areas of my life that may no longer be necessary to do? What do I need to adjust? Where have I tried to strive, or maybe overachieved unnecessarily in order to see things grow? What things have I taken the reins of, that God was meant to be holding? What am I to take hold of now?'

Ask God to speak to you about what adjustments you need to make and let the revelation of these changes be your saving grace. The good news is, that in the COVID-19 season and in every season, God is still in control.

Pray: 'God what now? What do You want me to do differently? What now for my family, my ministry, my business, my church, my future? What now? Holy Spirit, help me to hear what you are saying in this season that is causing us to be still? Amen'.

Write down what the Holy Spirit reveals to you, because let me tell you, it will be gold. It will be what you need going into the future.

# Part 4: YOUR STORY

# 16
ADJUSTING YOUR SAILS

We have identified a problem, and it's called 'control'. What about the solution? In this last section of my book, you are going to walk through some practical and spiritual steps you need to take in order to bring balance back into your life. Steps to move you from being the rescuer, and your 'fix it or lest we die', pattern of living; to simply doing what is actually helpful, fruitful or required by those involved.

Learning to leave in God's capable hands what you know, or what God shows you, you are not responsible for. Choosing to allow God to work unrestricted because you know He will bring a better result. Recognising that God sees the bigger picture in each situation and His desire for the bigger picture is to produce long lasting fruit. Understanding that the process will do a deep work which may cause the person or situation to seemingly get worse before it gets better, due to the fact that there is indeed, a deep work going on. Resting in the fact that God is doing His restorative surgery through the work of the Holy Spirit. Realising that for some situations, abandoning them completely to God alone is the only solution.

Finally, stand strong in the fact that prayer is our best weapon. Dedicated prayer, praying in the Holy Spirit and in the name of Jesus, the name above every other name; to God our loving Father who desires us to live a life according to His original intent. Genesis 1: 26-28 states that God created man in His image, His character, to rule and reign over all creation and live a whole and fruitful life.

**Question:** Are you ready to draw a line in the sand and take some serious steps towards wholeness?

If your answer is 'YES', and I hope it is, then understand it is going to take courage and vulnerability on your part, but also trust and complete surrender to God.

If you have said 'yes', then let's pray this prayer together today. Ask your heavenly Father, who loves you more than anything else in this world, to prove Himself faithful.

'Lord, I am committed to trusting You in this journey because You are fully trustworthy. Lord, I am choosing to believe that You are a good, good Father, because Your word says that if my son/daughter/mother/father/sister/brother/friend, asks me for bread, I would not give him/her a stone. I would not give him/her a snake, when he/she asked for a fish. I know You, who loves me much more than this, will only give good gifts to Your children. Lord, I know that You are God Almighty, and You alone, hold all things in Your hands. Today, I lay my life before You, Lord. I lay all my burdens and the burdens that I was never meant to carry, at Your feet. I recognise I need help. Restore me to wholeness so I can live my best life, not only for myself, but for others who are in my world. Amen'.

As you dive into this incredibly personal and valuable time with God, I ask that you do not rush through each step. This is not a task to complete, nor a race to win. It is not you orchestrating something to fix the situation, like in your default past. It is a journey, and as in any journey, you will find there are certain places on the path where you will need to just stop for a while.

It is time to admit to yourself that this whole process of trying to control everything in and around your life has worn you out. The good news is, God has the perfect answer for you.

Matthew 11:28-30 (MSG): 'Are you tired? Worn out? Burned out on religion? (exhausted by control – my addition) Come to me. Get away with me and you'll recover your life. I'll show you how to take a real rest. Walk with me and work with me - watch how I do it. Learn the unforced rhythms of grace. I won't lay anything heavy or ill-fitting on you. Keep company with me and you'll learn to live freely and lightly'.

What an amazing promise. Just reading this should cause you to sigh with relief.

# 17
## YOUR TOOL KIT

You will need a tool kit for your journey. Here are the tools you will need.

### THE HOLY SPIRIT

The most important tool you carry with you on this journey is the Holy Spirit. You cannot travel this road without Him. The Holy Spirit is your guide, your comforter and your encourager. He is patient and kind. He will wait with you for as long as it takes at each point. He will walk beside you every step of the way and you will hear Him whisper, 'Keep going, you can do this'.

### TIME

As you venture along this path, you may need to stop for a while because a deeper work of restoration needs to be done. That is ok. For us control people, stopping is easier said than done. Believe me, I know. We just want to do the steps, complete it, and get on with the next thing. It's almost like we are saying, 'Give me a quick download directly into my character so I can move on'. However, like I said, this is not your time to *fix*, this is your time for God, through the power of the Holy Spirit to *restore* you. To fix something means to repair a broken piece. It can be done in a very short time. Even if you like to repair something well, it often doesn't take too long, but you will always know it is a repair job. Restoring something is a different process. You take that broken piece, consider how it was initially created, then work on it until it is back to its original condition. This takes time, patience and effort, but you come out whole. What would you prefer? Restoration is the key! It is a long term, deeper solution. Right?

You may need to rest a little while at each check point to re-evaluate how you are doing. This is not a time of judgment, but a place where you can take a good look at how well you are doing in moving towards wholeness. Don't condemn yourself if you slip up. It is easy to lapse back into old patterns, particularly if a serious situation comes up and you want to jump in and fix it. I have done it many a time. However, the difference is that now I have tasted God's way and it is much better. If you have found yourself regaining that black belt of control, unwind from the situation and apologise, if necessary. Yep, humility may be needed. If it is too late for that particular situation, pick yourself up, don't punish yourself, repent for taking on Jesus' role, and move on.

### PEOPLE
For me, I only realised how broken I was when I was made aware of it. It took a pastor/ counsellor friend to tell me. As I shared in my story, it was he who pastored me, counselled me, checked in on me and encouraged me. My husband was also very understanding and patient as the Lord restored me. Don't be ashamed to ask for help. Choose only a select few who will love you through it, to be a life source for you in the process. Watch out for those who will take from you. Even those who may be of 'good intention' by telling you what you should do. This is not helpful. There is a difference between those who encourage and give you food for thought that lead you to a healthier way of thinking, and those who just want to help fix you. Find your Aarons and Hurs.

## TRUST

*Proverbs 3:5 (MSG): 'Trust God from the bottom of your heart; don't try to figure out everything on your own. Listen for God's voice in everything you do, everywhere you go; He's the one who will keep you on track. Don't assume that you know it all'.*

There will be times through the process of letting go, when you will be tempted to jump in and take over again. You will look at the issue that you have so faithfully committed to God, and see that it has become seemingly worse, not better. When I say seemingly worse, it is because we can only see physically the outworking of that situation. We cannot see what God is doing in the supernatural. *Don't assume that you know it all.*

Our job is to do what God requires us to do; no more, no less. One of the most valuable and effective tools you hold in your hands is the Word of God. The enemy doesn't want you to know the power that you hold in your hands. Yes, there is a battle to be won, whether that be small or insurmountable, but God is never taken by surprise by any situation or blunder.

Don't just believe me, believe what the Word of God says:

> *Job 34:21 (NKJV): 'For His eyes are upon the ways of a man, and He sees all his steps'.*

> *Psalm 33:13-15 (NKJV): 'The Lord looks from Heaven, He sees all the sons of men, from His dwelling place He looks out on all the inhabitants of the earth. He who fashions the hearts of them all, He who understands all their works'.*

> *Psalm 139: 2-3 (NASB): 'You know when I sit down and when I rise up. You understand my thought from afar. You scrutinize my path and my lying down, and You are intimately acquainted with all my ways'.*

*Jeremiah 23:24 (NASB): 'Can a man hide himself in hiding places, so I do not see him?' declares the Lord. 'Do I not fill the heavens and the earth?' declares the Lord'.*

*Psalm 139: 1-2 (NASB): 'O Lord, You have searched me and known me. You know when I sit down and when I rise up. You understand my thoughts from afar'.*

*Proverbs 15:3 (NASB): 'The eyes of the Lord are in every place, watching the evil and the good'.*

NOW YOU HAVE YOUR TOOL KIT IN HAND, LET'S BEGIN.

# 18
## BALANCE AND TRUST

## PEACE IN YOUR POSITION

I want you to start by listening to the song, 'Be Still', by Hillsong. The first words of this song say, 'Be still and know, that the Lord is in control'. As you listen to this song, open your heart to allow the Holy Spirit to speak to you. If you do that, HE WILL SPEAK.

> You can find this song on YouTube here:
> https://www.youtube.com/watch?v=H7pJb49vVQY
>
> (Note: You can legally listen to this here online but cannot legally download it)

After listening to this song, write down what God is saying to you. Firstly, start with what the Holy Spirit is revealing to you personally in the opening words of the song.

Be Still and know, that the Lord is in control. Taken from Psalm 46:10

..................................................................................................

..................................................................................................

..................................................................................................

..................................................................................................

..................................................................................................

..................................................................................................

Listen to the song again. Write down anything else that comes to mind, trusting the Holy Spirit is leading your thoughts.

..................................................................................................

..................................................................................................

..................................................................................................

..................................................................................................

..................................................................................................

..................................................................................................

## TRUSTING IN THE POWER OF GOD'S VOICE

The Bible's opening chapter, Genesis 1, reveals the unmatched, awesome power of God's ability.

*Genesis 1:3 And God said, 'Let there be light', and there was light. Verses 6-8: Then God said, 'Let there be a space between the waters, to separate the waters of the heavens from the waters of the earth. And that is what happened. God made this space to separate the waters of the earth from the waters of the heavens. God called the space sky'. Verse 11: Then God said, 'Let the land sprout with vegetation – every sort of seed-bearing plant, and trees that grow seed-bearing fruit. These seeds will then produce the kinds of plants and trees from which they came'. And that is what happened. Verses 26-30: Then God said, 'Let us make human beings in our image, to be like us. They will reign over the fish in the sea, the birds in the sky, the livestock, all the wild animals on the earth, and the small animals that scurry along the ground'. So God created human beings in His own image. In the image of God He created them; male and female He created them. Then God blessed them and said, 'Be fruitful and multiply. Fill the earth and govern it. Reign over the fish in the sea, the birds in the sky, and all the animals that scurry along the ground'. Then God said, 'Look! I have given you every seed-bearing plant throughout the earth and all the fruit trees for your food. And I have given every green plant as food for all the wild animals, the birds in the sky, and the small animals that scurry along the ground – everything that has life'. And that is what happened.*

God just has to speak the word and what He says, comes into being. Nothing is too difficult for Him.

# GOD'S VOICE CAUSES EVEN POWERFUL THINGS TO BE SHAKEN

*Psalm 29:1-11:* 'Ascribe to the Lord, you heavenly beings, ascribe to the Lord glory and strength. Ascribe to the Lord the glory due his name; worship the Lord in the splendour of his holiness. The voice of the Lord is over the waters; the God of glory thunders, the Lord thunders over the mighty waters. The voice of the Lord is powerful; the voice of the Lord is majestic. The voice of the Lord breaks the cedars; the Lord breaks in pieces the cedars of Lebanon. He makes Lebanon leap like a calf, Sirion like a young wild ox. The voice of the Lord strikes with flashes of lightning. The voice of the Lord shakes the desert; the Lord shakes the Desert of Kadesh. The voice of the Lord twists the oaks and strips the forests bare. And in his temple all cry, 'Glory!' The Lord sits enthroned over the flood; the Lord is enthroned as King forever. The Lord gives strength to His people; the Lord blesses His people with peace'.

Maybe you have read these two scriptures numerous times, particularly Genesis 1. However, whether this be the first time, or the one hundredth time, don't just read it, let God's truth about these verses sink in and get into your belief system.

If God's voice is all it takes to create the universe, move mountains, shake deserts, split strong cedar trees, make the blind to see and the lame to walk, turn water into wine, create mankind, and not least of all, raise Christ from the dead; what does it say about His qualifications and ability to work in your situation?

In light of understanding how able our God is, reflect on how you have automatically defaulted to your control nature and tried to 'fix', 'rescue', 'orchestrate', 'defend', in order for your world and everyone in your world, to not fall apart.

## THE WHY?

What do you believe is the root cause of your needing to control? Be completely honest with yourself. Remember, this interactive section of the book is between you and God. You know that God knows the answer already, correct? Don't sugar coat it. Get real with yourself and with God. Allow the Holy Spirit to bring it to the surface, and then write it down. There is something powerful about writing down what is stuffed deep in your soul. Chains will break, truth will be revealed and healing will come.

..................................................................................................

..................................................................................................

..................................................................................................

..................................................................................................

..................................................................................................

..................................................................................................

..................................................................................................

## REACT VS RESPOND ROAD MAP

I have an exercise for you to do. It is called the 'React vs Respond Road Map'. This roadmap is all about responding to a situation rather than reacting to it.

It is a practical exercise where you will lay out exactly what is happening in your world. It will help you identify where you jump in and try and be God in a situation.

### THERE ARE FOUR THINGS YOU NEED TO DO IN PREPARATION.

### PAUSE
The first thing you need to do is pause. Yes, that's right, pause. Why? Because us 'black belt' control people don't want to wait. We draw our swords, jump in and before you know it, we have cut someone's ear off and they may have not even been involved in the situation in the first place. Whoops!

### BREATHE
You may be thinking, 'Isn't this the same thing as pause?' The answer is no. It is definitely not. Taking a deep breath will lower stress levels in your body and sends messages to your brain to calm down and relax. Some of us need to take several breaths, but you have to do it. What *is* the same as pause though, is that taking a deep breath gives you time to gather your thoughts to make a rational decision.

### DECIDE
This is where you consider which road you are going to take. Are you going to default to your control scenario where you allow yourself to be led by your emotions and the urge to take over? Or are you going to choose the better way, where God has room to move? The decision is yours. I hope you choose the latter, where you draw a line in the sand, and do not cross that boundary line. Be responsible for what you are required to be responsible for, and no more. Be aware of 'guilt responsibility'. What I mean by guilt responsibility is assuming in your mind

that an expectation has been put on you, or even has been alluded to by others, to do more than your part. The decision you choose will not only affect you, but everyone around you. Remember, God is more than able to do what you leave in His hands.

## DEFINE

The path you choose by the decisions you make, will define you, and the life you will want to live from this point on.

The next three pages contain three 'React vs Respond' Road Maps. The first one is the outline of what you need to do in order to create your own road map. The second one, is my personal React vs Respond Road Map. Here you get to see how I have done mine. As you will see, it is just the main points. The third one is for you to fill out. You may want to copy this several times for several different situations. You could create a big one to put up on a wall somewhere as a reminder. You may also find that you need a separate journal to write down the many things that have been building up in your heart over a long period of time.

*Note: This particular road map has been taken from the Life Skills program 'Flourish', which I co-wrote with Bek Windsor. This is copyright material but you have permission to copy this roadmap for your own personal use only.*
*Thank you.*

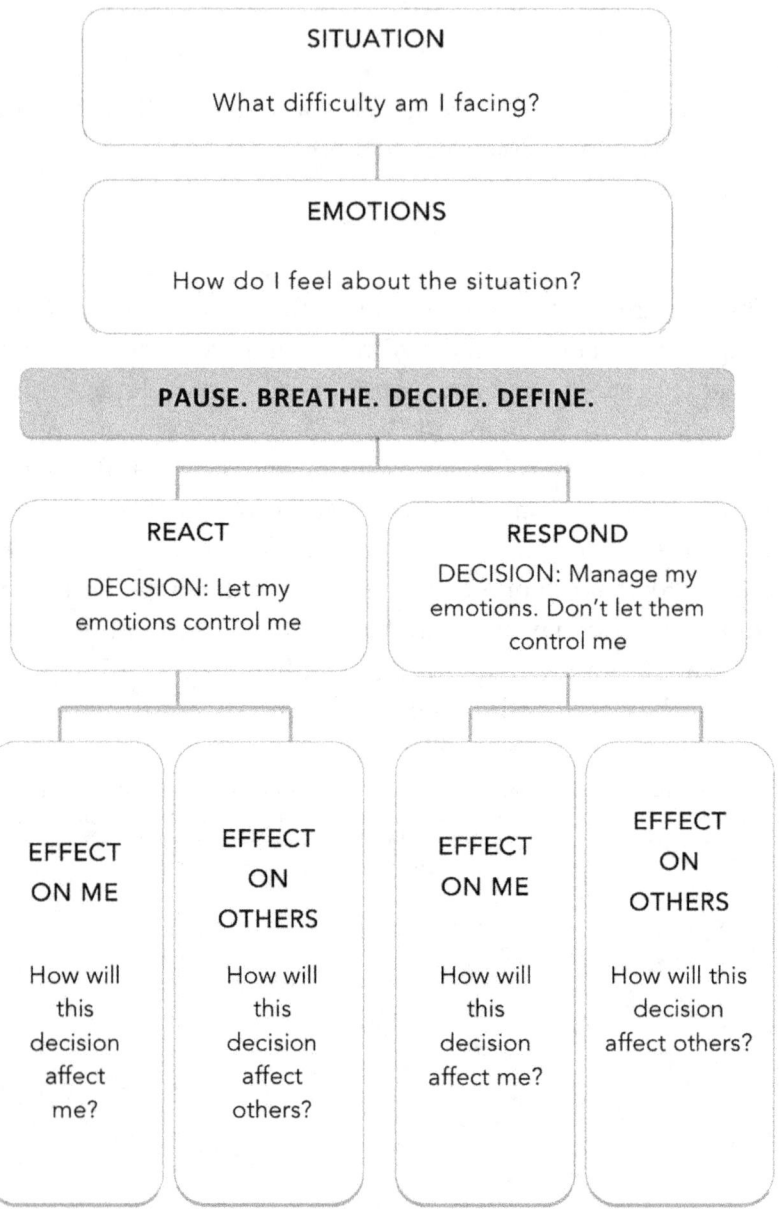

# Deb's REACT vs RESPOND ROAD MAP

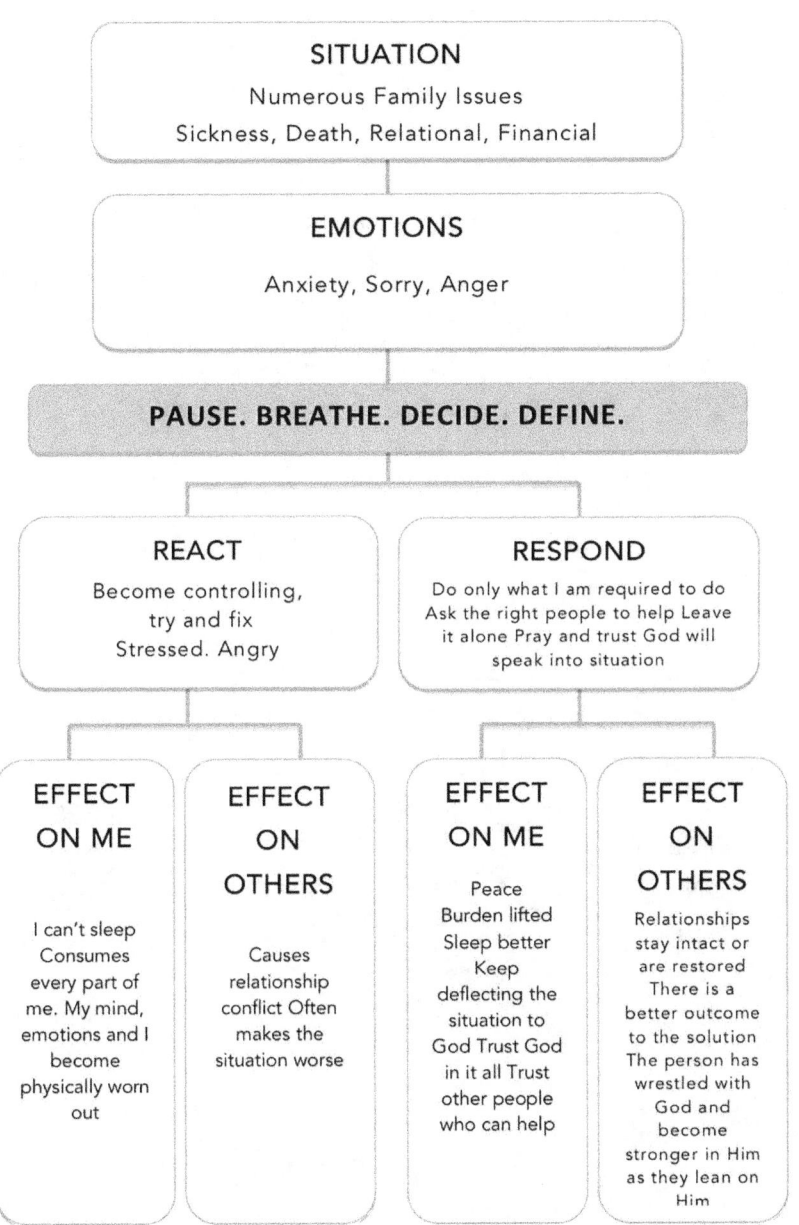

# Your **REACT vs RESPOND ROAD MAP**

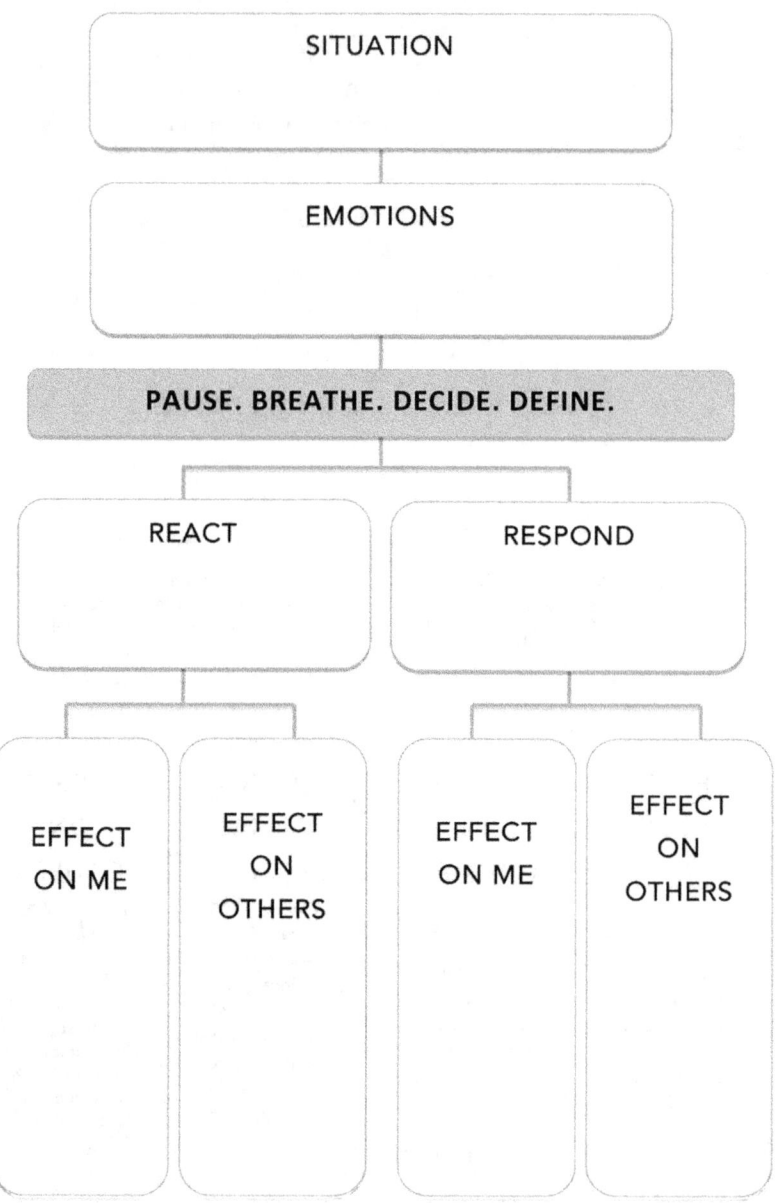

After doing this exercise, what have you discovered about yourself and the way you have been handling situations in your life?

..................................................................................
..................................................................................
..................................................................................
..................................................................................
..................................................................................
..................................................................................
..................................................................................
..................................................................................

What are some things you can put in place to help your default response to be dropping to your knees first? What steps will you take to give control back to God and allow Him to be your burden carrier?

..................................................................................
..................................................................................
..................................................................................
..................................................................................
..................................................................................
..................................................................................
..................................................................................

'Come to Me, all you who labor and are heavy laden, and I will give you rest. Take My yoke upon you and learn from Me, for I am gentle and lowly in heart, and you will find rest for your souls. For My yoke is easy and My burden is light'. Matthew 11:28-30 (NKJV).

Jesus will remove your heavy burden of guilt and hopelessness and replace it with peace and rest in Him.

## GOD'S PROMISES

'For I, the Lord your God, will hold your right hand, saying to you, Fear not, I will help you'. Isaiah 41:13 (NKJV). God promises to support and help you through every trial.

'Therefore, humble yourselves under the mighty hand of God, that He may exalt you in due time, casting all your care upon Him, for He cares for you'. 1 Peter 5:6-7 (NKJV). Just knowing your heavenly Father cares about you personally can make any load seem lighter.

'Even to your old age, I am He, and even to gray hairs I will carry you! I have made, and I will bear; even I will carry, and will deliver you'. Isaiah 46:4 (NKJV). The Lord desires to constantly support you throughout your life, with the intention of saving you eternally.

'He will feed His flock like a shepherd; He will gather the lambs with His arm, and carry them in His bosom'. Isaiah 40:11 (NKJV). The Good Shepherd will gladly bear you in His gentle arms right now.

'The righteous cry out, and the Lord hears, and delivers them out of all their troubles'. Psalm 34:17 (NKJV). If you belong to Him, God will always listen when you call to Him for help.

'In the beginning was the word'. John 1:1 (NKJV). The Word. In Genesis 1, we read that all God needed to do was speak a word and things came into existence. That is the power of God's voice. That is the power of the Word of God.

'The voice of the Lord shakes the wilderness'. Psalm 29:8 (NKJV). Read the whole of Psalm 29. It is powerful. It has been one of my favourite scriptures while going through the journey of handing things over to Jesus.

'I will cry to you when my heart is overwhelmed'. Psalm 61:2 (NKJV). When we have no words, God still understands our cry.

## DON'T SKIP THE EPILOGUE

When an unhealthy desire to control situations is your default, you are taking on a role that was never meant to be yours. It really comes down to choosing to fully trust God rather than relying on your own ability to turn things around.

Laying your control issue at the Father's feet is the easy part. The most difficult decision is not picking it back up as soon as you walk out of His throne room.

Your decision to trust God is not a natural human response, but it is a natural supernatural response. We are not just fleshly beings, but are spirit also. Our flesh, the vehicle we get around in, feels pain, anxiety, burden, joy and laughter. However, the things of the flesh will not sustain us. It is in the unseen part of us where God is at work, both in us, and working for us. It is in the unseen world where God releases an army of angels to come and fight for us. It is in the unseen world where Jesus petitions the Father on our behalf to change hearts, reveal truths, open doors, and close them. It is in the unseen world where God birthed every day of your life and the lives of those around you. Nothing ever takes Him by surprise.

Through the whisper of the Holy Spirit living within us, He speaks gently and yet decisively. Listen for it. It is in this place He reveals these deeper revelations into our own spirit, which gives us confidence and peace to move forward, allowing God to take the reins. Be assured, that He has everything under control.

*'Which of you, if your son asks for bread, will give him a stone? Or if he asks for a fish, will give him a snake? If you, then, though you are evil, know how to give good gifts to your children, how much more will your Father in heaven give good gifts to those who ask Him!'* Matthew 7:9-11

I pray that you have gained some tools in order to walk only with the burden that Christ has put on you to bear. The light and easy one. Jesus is our heavy burden carrier. The Holy Spirit will guide you into all truth, and give you peace.

## ABOUT THE AUTHOR

Deborah is a long-term missionary who has been ministering alongside her husband Paul in South East Asia for over twenty years. Together they now also minister globally.

Deborah has a passion to see men and women of all ages rise up and pursue the call of God on their lives and become an influence in their own world. Deborah is also an author, speaker and the co-developer of 'Flourish', a life skills program for women which is now running in over 30 nations.

Her best achievement is being a wife to her husband Paul, a mother to her two grown children, and a nan to seven amazing grand babies.

## BOOKS

**Just Say YES**
Available at: Koorong bookstores and Koorong online.
Available at: iTunes, Amazon and Kobo as an e-book

**Out of Control**
Available at: https://www.facebook.com/IsayYES/
Available at: iTunes, Amazon and Kobo as an e-book

## LIFESKILLS
**Flourish Life Skills Program for women of all ages.**
Co-developers: Deborah Hilton and Bek Windsor
Website: http://keystoneintl.org

## AVAILABLE TO SPEAK
Contact Deb @ deborahhilton101@gmail.com

## CONNECT
Follow me on Facebook @ https://www.facebook.com/IsayYES/
Email @ deborahhilton101@gmail.com

REFERENCES

Joanna
https://www.biblegateway.com/resources/all-women-bible/Joanna
http://www.womeninthebible.net/women-bible-old-new-testaments/joanna/

Supergirl: Viewing the movie on YouTube

React vs Respond Roadmap: Flourish Life Skills Program, Keystone International Inc. Included with permission of Keystone International.

Laughter: Authors: Lawrence Robinson, Melinda Smith, M.A., and Jeanne Segal, Ph.D. Last updated: November 2019.
https://www.helpguide.org/articles/mental-health/laughter-is-the-best-medicine.htm